BROKEN to GRACE

PATRICIA S. QUILLEN

© 2014 Kingdom Builders Publications
Patricia S. Quillen

All rights reserved. No part of this book may be reproduced or transmitted in any form or by any means without written permission from the author.
Printed in the USA
ISBN 9780578143859
Library of Congress Control Number 2014949084

Scripture References by BibleGateway.com
KJV
NKJV
KJV21
HCSB
AKJV
NLT
NIV
AMP
ESV

Authored
Patricia S. Quillen

Edited by
Nichole Smith
Louise Smith
KBPublications

Photographer
LH Photography "Just Pose"

Cover Design
Kwonyah Designs
Mark Linen
LoMar Designs

This book belongs to

DEDICATION

I want to give thanks to my Lord and Savior Jesus Christ for giving me the ability to put my thoughts into words by telling my story.

This book is dedicated in memory of my parents Bobbie and Joe Woods. They left their hand prints on my heart with their un-ending love and grace.

To my adorable husband Jacob Quillen, JR - thank you for praying for me, and supporting me on this journey. I love the God in you. Thank you for pushing me to become all that God has created me to be and for walking with beside me.

To my children and grandchildren, Shawn, Monica, Kayden, Brittany, Mckayla, AShon, and Jaheem; My siblings, Cynthia , Betty, Gregory. My Aunt Jessie and Uncle David, thank you all for your love and support.

Dr. Carl Morris; my pastor, friend, supporter and encourager; Pastor Carl gives me spiritual insight and endless motivation to unleash the power God has place inside of me.

To Associate Pastor Steve Osborne; thank you Pastor Steve for your support and encouragement to follow God and my heart. you are one of my biggest fans!

 Thanks to you Dr. Tommy Burbage for your professionalism, encouragement, support and editing of my daily devotions.

Mrs. Barbara Godwin, my friend, encourager and supporter.

To Mrs. Tina McCormick Esaw, a good friend and co-worker; thank you for listening to my devotions almost every morning before the start of our work day.

Hats off to you Kingdom Builders Publications, LLC for your support and demonstrating the love of God with excellence!!

CONTENTS

DEDICATION iii

PREFACE ix

INTRODUCTION xi

Chapter 1 12

    911 EMERGENCY 12

    I BELONG TO YOU 15

    BLOOM WHERE YOU'RE PLANTED 18

    LEARNING TO LOVE YOURSELF 21

    THE BLESSING LIES IN YOUR DECISION 24

Chapter 2 27

    CRUSHED, BUT STILL STANDING 27

    MY FATHER IS FAITHFUL 30

    CLAIM YOUR INHERITANCE 33

    I REACHED A TURNING POINT 36

    A HEART ISSUE 39

CHAPTER 3 42

    DISCONNECT TO CONNECT 42

    RIGHT THINKING PRODUCES, RIGHT BEHAVIOR 45

    SWEET REVELATION 47

I OWN MY FAITH 49

A GODLY MOTHER IS A GIFT FROM GOD 51

CHAPTER 4 55

ATTRIBUTES OF A MATURE CHRISTIAN 55

PEACE 57

God's Masterpiece 60

HEED THE CALL 62

Chapter 5 65

THORNS 65

UNLOCK YOUR GOD-GIVEN POTENTIAL 67

LISTENING WITH A PURPOSE 71

FACE TO FACE WITH THE ENEMY 74

CHAPTER 6 77

HEAVEN OR HELL? THE CHOICE IS YOURS! 77

PREREQUISET FOR LOVING 79

WE HAVE NOTHING TO FEAR BUT FEAR IN SELF 82

MY FIRST LOVE 85

Chapter 7 88

TEAR DOWN TO REBUILD 88

Are you a visionary? 91

COME LORD JESUS COME 94

MAXIMIZE GOD'S PRECIOUS GIFT OF TIME 96

GOD REQUIRE FAITHFULNESS 99

Chapter 8 101

DIFFICULT TIMES PRODUCES GODLY CHARACTER 101

ARE YOUR FRUIT BRUISED OR ROTTEN? 104

THE TRUST FACTOR 107

A PINK TORNADO 110

Chapter 9 112

PEACE BE STILL 112

LORD, HELP MY UNBELIEF 115

GOOGLE DOES NOT HAVE ALL THE ANSWERS 118

HOW BIG IS YOUR GOD? 121

DILIGENCE IS A GOD THING 123

CHAPTER 10 127

FULFILL YOUR MINISTRY 127

THIS PLACE 130

OBEDIENCE IS BETTER THAN A SACRIFICE 132

A CLUTTERED MIND 135

THE OLD IS FAMILIAR BUT NEW IS BETTER 138

Chapter 11 141

PRAYER FOR SPIRITUAL INSIGHT 141

CAN THESE BONES LIVE? 143

DON'T WORRY, BE HAPPY? 146

IN OUR HEAVENLY FATHER, WE HAVE HOPE 149

A SECRET STORM 152

MISSION IMPOSSIBLE 155

ABOUT THE AUTHOR 157

PREFACE

I remember sitting at my desk early this particular Tuesday morning, January 7, 2014 excited about a new year. I was anticipating a great day when my phone began buzzing and my computer gave out a long ring indicating an email was just received. I along with 28 other people received the same email. It started off.... "Good Morning Everyone!" Now, usually when I get an email that starts out, "Good Morning Everyone!" I quickly put it in a category and drag it to the bottom of the computer screen then gently slam dunk it in the trash can, but this was a different kind of "Good Morning Everyone!" It urged me to read on. The greeting was followed by the words I had just prayed... "I am so thankful for God's Mercy and His awesome Grace that He gives me daily. What a wonderful Father and Friend we have in Jesus." The email was crammed full of gratitude for what Jesus has done for humanity. I was so uplifted when I read, "Nothing you or I will ever do will take God by surprise. The Lord does not see us as cast outs, or not good enough, but He sees all of his children beautifully and wonderfully made." I knew I was reading the truth when I got to the sentence that said, "....we are a work in progress." That statement made me feel complete in Jesus. So many times, when we stumble and make mistakes, we struggle in our ability to stand back up and start walking again; not anymore because I understand I am a work in progress. As a matter of fact, I believe I am Heaven's HUGE undertaking. God has His hands full with me! I trust Him to complete the good work He started in me. He is more than capable of completing it. It will probably take me a life time for His masterpiece to be completed in my life.

The email ended with a challenge for the year.... "Stay in the word, pray and allow God to begin a NEW WORK in you this NEW YEAR." Signed, Pat Quillen.

That email was a wonderful way to have started my day and my New Year. Since that Tuesday morning, I have received an email from Pat every day. I look forward to receiving my morning encouragement and am keenly aware that God is thinking about me and involved in my day. Pat has a way of breathing life into her past and present experiences, both the good and the broken through her ability to tell a story. The devotions in this book are relatable and may remind you of a time in your past but they will always speak to your present. I encourage you to grab a cup coffee, find a quiet place, and enjoy a Grace Filled Devotion to start your day. yours for Abundant Life...evermore,

Steve Osborn,
Executive Pastor
Abundant Life Church

INTRODUCTION

This book is birth from my personal life experiences, challenges and struggles. I have a deep desire to help others discover their God given potential. I pray that Broken to Grace will give insight into the heart and mind of God through these simple and practical ways. In your reading I have incorporated scripture that will help you get to know God better; and in the process you can begin to heal from the inside out. My prayer is that you will discover, you are not your past, your failures and what others have said you are. I pray this devotional will show you how to avoid obstacles that have stunted your growth in the past. Life is more than your daily agenda, hurrying to work, and carpooling, making dinner, assisting the kids with homework, and doing household chores. While all that is important, there is more to life. For too long in my life, I have existed and not lived. We have God's word that promises our latter days can be better than our beginning. However when I received the revelation of God's love for me, my life was forever changed. God's desire is for us to live life in abundance, in peace, love and happiness. It is never too late to start over with the help of our loving and caring Father. In the heart of my stories are promises from God's word to inspire and motivate you to change your perspective and see yourself through the eyes of a loving and caring Father. By experiencing the Lord's awesome power, His unconditional love and acceptance, I believe your life will never be the same. *Jeremiah 1:5 says, (KJV) 5Before I formed thee in the belly I knew thee; and before thou camest forth out of the womb I sanctified thee, and I ordained thee a prophet unto the nations.*

Patricia

Chapter 1

911 EMERGENCY

Hello and thank you for calling; someone will be with you shortly. I have heard that statement more times than I care to recall. What if - just what if we call God and He said, "Hold on, I will be with you shortly." you waited on the other end of the line and you heard complete silence; or you held on so long; you finally hung up. Now that you are aggravated and humiliated you decide to hang up and call back. Now your call is immediately forwarded to voice mail! Hum! Every time we choose not to pray, not to read our bible or not to talk to God, we are leaving a voice mail message. It goes like this, "Lord I do not have time for you today. I have other obligations and commitments. I am late for an appointment. I have a million things to do today and you are not in my plans... I will talk to you later." You are in essence saying, "Lord, your dying was in vain." Nothing is more important than spending time with God. **Jeremiah 31:3ᵇ, (KJV)** *I have loved you with an everlasting love.* It doesn't matter how far you try to run from God, He loves you and wants to forgive you of your sins. He created you and cares about you. We have all done, thought or said bad things, which the Bible calls "sin." **Romans 3:23 (KJV)** *All have sinned and fall short of the glory of God.*

God is teaching me how to walk intimately with Him. His Holy Spirit is assisting and maturing me in the things of God. Remember, life is a journey and none of us have arrived. As a church goer, I attended church on Sunday, gambled and partied the rest of the week. I thought as long as I attend church most of the time, God understood. I wore so many different masks; I could hardly tell who I was. I took so many things for granted; today I realize life is precious. Knowing about God and having an intimate relationship with Him are not the same. I am so grateful to God for saving me, and thankful today, that I have an intimate relationship with Him. I want to challenge you, to live each day as if it is your last. Tomorrow is not promised and today is truly a gift. We will encounter trials, and disappointments, but this life is temporary. ***James 1:2-4 (NKJV)*** *²Count it all joy, my brothers, when you meet trials of various kinds, for you know that the testing of your faith produces steadfastness. And let steadfastness have its full effect, that you may be perfect and complete, lacking in nothing.* For those of us that have our faith and hope in God, we are working to have eternal life with our Heavenly Father. Do not grow weary. Jesus was persecuted, so why not you? ***James 1:12 (KJV)*** *"Blessed is the man who remains steadfast under trial, for when he has stood the test he will receive the crown of life, which God has promised to those who love Him.*

God's desire is to have a close, intimate, personal, and powerful relationship, with His children. Christianity is not about our weekly church attendance, or how much money we pay. We must move to another level in God. The deeper our personal relationship is with God the more the devil is fearful of us. We are called to be a light in a dark world. People are masking hurt, and smiling through their tears. We desperately need to get serious about our Father's business. One day we are going to have to give an account of our life here on this earth. How will you be remembered? ***Hebrews 10:22 (NKJ)*** *Let us draw near to God with a sincere heart in full assurance of faith, having our hearts* *sprinkled to cleanse us from a guilty conscience and having our bodies washed with pure water.* God wants imperfect people with a willing mind and open heart. Thank you Lord for loving us. We can't earn salvation; we are saved by God's grace when we have faith in His Son, Jesus Christ. All you have to do is believe you are a sinner and that Christ died for your sins and ask His forgiveness. What matters to God is the attitude of our hearts and our honesty.

PRAYER
✶✶✶✶✶

Thank you Lord for this new and exciting day. Thank you Father for dying on the cross for a sinner like me. Lord there is nothing more important than spending intimate time with you. Lord, forgive us for putting other things ahead of you. Lord, teach us how to seek you more. Lord create in us a pure heart, and renew a right Spirit within us. Father, thank you for your divine mercy and grace. Lord we love you and long to be in your will. Father in you Lord we have freedom and liberty to be what you desire us to be. In Jesus mighty name, Amen.

I BELONG TO YOU

William McDowell pens the exact sentiment of my heart in his song, I belong to you, my life is not my own; to you I belong. Lord I belong to you, ever fiber within me belongs to you.

Looking back on my life, I am so thankful that God has allowed me to get to this place. ***Psalm 100:5*** *(NKJV) For the LORD is good; his mercy is everlasting; and his truth endureth to all generations.* The more intimately I get with God, the more I long to know about Him. We should have a zeal and - an eagerness to learn what makes our God happy. The mind and heart of God is revealed to us in His word.

Psalm 119:10 (NKJV) *With my whole heart have I sought thee: O let me not wander from thy commandments.* When I met my wonderful husband, I was immediately attracted to him physically. However his demeanor and his spiritual insight made me want to know more about him as a person. We began dating and learning more about each other. Everything about him interested me. The more time I spend getting to know him, the more time I desired to spend with him. I acted as a detective undercover. We knew some of the same people so I would ask our mutual acquaintances about his character. Our Lord and Savior is no different. In order to have a relationship with God, we must invest time with Him to learn of His character. Our God is awesome. He is faithful and true. God's character has been proven from the beginning of time. He is authentic. His track record is excellent and without blemish. ***Psalm 34:8***

(NKJV) *Taste and see that the LORD is good; blessed is the man who takes refuge in him.* God is good and He is good all the time and His character never changes.

When trouble is on every side, seek God. When you are faced with an important decision, and just don't know what to do, pray. God said He will never leave us nor will He forsake us. God is GOOD and He will never let you down. The Lord is Holy and righteous; meaning whatever He does is right and perfect. **Romans 11:33 (KJV)** *Oh, the depth of the riches both of the wisdom and knowledge of God! How unsearchable are His judgments and His ways past finding out!*

When situations and circumstances do not turn out the way I want them to, it gives me comfort to know that the God I serve is Holy and righteous and has the answer, plan and direction I should take. Strive for intimacy with God. He is good all the time. Some situations you will encounter in life will cause you to wonder, where is God in this?

Proverbs 15:3 (NKJV) *His eyes are in every place, The eyes of the LORD are in every place, keeping watch on the evil and the good.* Everything that our Lord and Savior has promised to you and me, He will bring to pass. Have you ever walked in a dark room and could not see anything, but when you turn the light on, all is well? Without God, we are walking in darkness, but when we come to know God, our lives become brighter. It is not enough for us to know about God; we must get to know God intimately. We get to know God better when we face trials, tribulations and struggles. I encourage you not to hate or despise trials as that is where your character and strength comes. Our God is omniscient. God knows everything and His knowledge is complete. When the storms of life are raging, you've got to know whose you are and where your help comes from. We belong to God. He paid the ultimate sacrifice on the cross for you and me.

❋(PRAYER)❋
✽✽✽✽✽✽

Lord, this is the day you have made, and I will rejoice and be glad in it. Father, thank you for being so good to me. Lord, your awesomeness never ceases to amaze me. Lord, I belong to you and all that I am and ever hope to be is because of you. Lord, every day I see your hand at work in my life. When I think of you and your goodness, it brings a smile to my face and puts joy in my heart. Lord, when I feel my heart beat, I am reminded how close you are to me. Father God, you bring me so much peace and hope. Thank you Lord for loving me and making me the person that you want me to be. Lord, your desires are my desires and I know that you Oh Lord know what is best for me. Lord, every day I look forward to our special time together. Lord, I am so thankful that I can talk to you anytime and anywhere. Lord, I am thankful for all that you are to me. In your precious name, Amen.

BLOOM WHERE YOU'RE PLANTED

Have you ever said to yourself, "When I get another job...", or "When I can afford it...", or "When the time presents itself...I will do this or that"? I have. Now what if that time never comes? We have to be adaptable to changing times and circumstances. The time is now! Time waits on no one. Each new day is a gift from our almighty God and we should treat it as the gift that it is. **Matthew 6:34 (KJV)** *Therefore do not worry about tomorrow, for tomorrow will worry about its own things. Sufficient for the day is its own trouble.* Living our lives one day at a time is what the Lord requires from each of us. Concentrate on one challenge at a time as they occur. Having this mind set, will enable us to refrain from worrying about what tomorrow may bring. Know that no weapon formed against you will prosper.

Psalm 118:29 (NKJV) *Oh, give thanks to the LORD, for He is good! For His mercy endures forever.* We all have busy life styles, and much to do. It is easy to get off course and into the future. The word of God is clear that we should stay in today and tomorrow will take care of itself. We don't know if we will be alive tomorrow, but God has everything in His hands and He is the only one that knows what tomorrow will bring. If you knew you only had 30 days to live, what would you do differently? I want to challenge you to not put off what you can do today, with the help of God. Whatever your answer may be, it should reflect how you are living your life at that very moment. The most important time frames are the minutes that make up each

God-given day. Happiness comes as we seize each moment. **Romans 15:17 (NKJV)** *Therefore I have reason to glory in Christ Jesus in the things which pertain to God.* God desires and commands for his people to be happy. Take hold of every opportunity.

II Corinthians 7:4 (NKJV) *Great is my boldness of speech toward you, and great is my boasting on your behalf. I am filled with comfort. I am exceedingly joyful in all our tribulation.*

We have to learn that when life give us lemons, make lemonade. When rain comes in our lives, learn to dance in it, and just know this too will pass. When you are having a challenging day, there is no need to burden those around you, give your problem to God. There is an old song that says, <u>Count your many blessings and see what the Lord has done.</u> I am too blessed to be stressed! We can handle any problem that comes our way if we will learn to take it to God in prayer and believe that our Heavenly Father will take care of it. Take a few minutes out of each day, pray and ask the Lord for His guidance and His peace. Prayer is vital for real happiness. It is as important as the pumping of your heart in order to live. **1 Peter 4:13 (NKJV)** *"but rejoice to the extent that you partake of Christ's sufferings, that when His glory is revealed, you may also be glad with exceeding joy.* Each day is filled with the goodness and wonders of God's glory. Enjoy this day! Every day is a new beginning!

❧PRAYER❧
✸✸✸✸✸✸

Thank you, Father God, for this day. Thank you for this moment. Lord I love you and my deepest desire is to live my life pleasing to you. Lord, this is the day you have made and I will rejoice and be glad in it. Father, help me to stay in today, because tomorrow is not promised to me. Thank you Lord for every heartbeat. Lord help me to live each day as if it is my last. Lord help me share a smile with someone that may be in need of a smile or a kind word. Father, help me to focus on you and your goodness and not worry about things I cannot change. Lord there is much to worry about if I would allow my mind to wonder, but I refuse to give that power over to the enemy. Psalm 119:105 tells me, (NKJV) "Thy word is a lamp unto my feet, and a light unto my path. "your Word, Father, I have hidden in my heart. In Jesus' precious name we pray, Amen.

LEARNING TO LOVE YOURSELF

If I ask you the question, "Do you like yourself?" I anticipate your response to be quite positive. I asked my co-worker that question and her answer was "Sure; emphatically!" She stated, "I love people, but I am not a people person." I was puzzled by her comment. My co-worker then stated when she and I met she felt comfortable with me. My co-worker also added that our relationship felt like an old familiar shoe. God desires to have a close and intimate relationship with us and to love on us as only God can. My belief is, if you are unable to love others, you are unable to love yourself. I remember, as a child, I wanted long hair; I desired to be taller and thinner. There are some things I can change and some I cannot. As I learned more things about God, His character and His love for me, I realized He accepts me the way I am. We tend to focus on our outer appearance, which is important, but God look on the heart of man. I know now that I am beautifully and wonderfully made. I am God's masterpiece. When we get to know God, and fall in love with Him, we can love ourselves and others. Take a moment and hug yourself; it is okay. When you really know how much God loves you, then you will focus your attention on the Creator of love.

James 2:8 (NKJV) *If you really fulfill the royal law according to the Scripture, you shall love your neighbor as yourself you do well…*

Leviticus 19:18 (NKJV) *you shall not take vengeance, nor bear any grudge against the children of your people, but you shall love your neighbor as yourself: I am the LORD.*

Every day and night my grandson, Kayden, will say to me "I love you Nana." I am not certain if he knows what love is, but because I tell him I love him, it has become a habit. That is something I want to ingrain in him, not only in words, but in my actions. I want him to know that I love him deeply. God wants His children to take His word at face value, and stop analyzing everything. Just believe! Take God at His Word. you are loved, unconditionally and always.

In order to love the people around us, we must first love ourselves. When we can accept the love that our Heavenly Father has for us, we can start to love ourselves. We can then begin to respect ourselves and live the life God died for us to enjoy fully. According to **Ephesians 5:29 (NKJV),** *you shall not take vengeance, nor bear any grudge against the children of your people, but you shall love your neighbor as yourself: I am the LORD.* Are you nourishing and carefully protecting yourself as God desires? Are you just existing instead of living your life in God's abundance? Every day, God shows His divine love to His children; have you recognized God's love for you today? I challenge you to STOP what you are doing and take a deep breath. Now, ask yourself whose air are you inhaling? Everything is about God's love for His children. It has already been bought and paid in full; just accept it. I realize some of us have been beat down in life, faced many obstacles and challenges, but we are still standing. We have so much to thank our God for.

John 3:16 (NKJV) *For God so loved the world that He gave His only begotten Son, that whosoever believes in Him should not perish but have everlasting life.*

Deuteronomy 6:5 (NKJV) *you shall love the LORD your God with all your heart, with all your soul, and with all your strength.*

We can express our love to God by spending time with Him and in His word, by telling God how much we love Him, by praising Him and being obedient to His Word. The love of God is on the inside of us; however, we should pass it on to others. Love is an action word. Remember you cannot give or offer to others what you do not possess.

PRAYER

Father, I am grateful for your love. I am so thankful for your unconditional devotion to me. Thank you for investing in me. Lord, I love you and desire to be in your will. Lord, create in me a pure heart and renew a right spirit within me. Lord, continue to give me a teachable spirit and a longing to live for you. Lord, I am still a work in progress, but I realize that you love me too much to leave me the way I am. Father, thank you for loving me in spite of my imperfections and flaws. Lord I realize, that only what I do for you will last. Lord, help me to be authentic in all that I do, so that it will bring you honor. Lord teach me how to love like you love. In Jesus' mighty name, I pray these things, Amen.

Patricia S. Quillen

THE BLESSING LIES IN YOUR DECISION

Everything starts with a thought, an idea and then a conscience decision. you are where you are in your life because of your decisions. Every right decision is based on the Word of God. When we choose not to consult God, we end up in a place we do not want to be.

According to **_Philippians 4:6-7 (NKJV)_** *6Be anxious for nothing, but in everything by prayer and supplication, with thanksgiving, let your requests be made known to God; 7and the peace of God, which surpasses all understanding, will guard your hearts and minds through Christ Jesus..*

We should be willing to submit to God, listen and obey His answer. It is imperative that our will become God's will. When your will is humbly and totally submitted to our Father, you can have confidence that He will lead the way. We should be ready to accept God's answer about any situation. From my experience, His answer is not always yes; sometimes, He tells us to wait, and other times His answer is No!

I know that God's will and desire for me is so much better than mine. Decision-making is a step-by-step process; we should be willing to invest time in God's Word and wait for His decision. Any decision I have made in haste, I have always regretted. For the most part, we make decisions based on our knowledge of the situation, our present and past experiences. Remember, we are human- beings; therefore, our knowledge is limited. When you are faced with a decision and seeking our God for the right answer, you will get a gut feeling deep down on the inside that I believe is one of God's way of saying, "Wait."

Proverbs 3:5-7 (NKJV) *5Trust in the Lord with all your heart, And lean not on your own understanding; 6In all your ways acknowledge Him, And He shall direct your paths. 7Do not be wise in your own eyes; Fear the Lord and depart from evil.*

Those with tunnel-vision, people who are locked into one way of thinking, are likely to miss the right road because they have closed their minds to any new options. We need the help of those who can enlarge our vision and broaden our perspectives. Seek out the advice of those who you know and trust that have a wealth of experience. Can you see the fruit of their labor? When we consult God, He will give us the right counsel. God wants us to plan, but include Him in our plans, and He will direct our steps. I have been praying about some situations for some time now. I have some important decisions to make, but I have learned not to move ahead of God. I attended a Women's Conference last evening, and the pastor talked about a pressing place. That is where I am right now. However, I realize more now it is for my good. This place does not feel good, but I know it is working for my good. The pressing place is where the Lord removes those toxins that can become poisonous and detrimental. **Proverbs 15:22 (21st Century King James KJ21)** *Without counsel purposes are disappointed: but in the multitude of counsellors they are established.*

Proverbs 15:15(NKJV) *All the days of the afflicted are evil, But he who is of a merry heart has a continual feast.* Our attitude depends on our ability to make good sound decisions. Our attitude colors our whole personality. We cannot always choose what happens to us, but we can choose our attitude toward that situation and the circumstances. A good man thinks before he speaks because he wants to say what he knows in the best possible way. The evil man doesn't wait to speak, because he doesn't care about the effects of his words. It is important to have something to say, but it is equally important to say it well. This is why we need to consult God.

Romans 8:28 (NKJV) *And we know that all things work together for good to them that love God, to them who are the called according to his purpose.* When making any decision, start by consulting the Heavenly Father. God works out all things, not just isolated incidents for our good. God's ultimate goal for us is to make us more like Christ! Yes, this also applies to our daily decision making. As we become more and more like Him, each of us will discover our true selves, the individuals we were meant to be.

✥ PRAYER ✥
✱✱✱✱✱

Father, thank you for this day. Thank you for loving me and seeing me as I will be. Oh Heavenly Father, thank you for departing your wisdom and understanding into my daily decision-making. Lord, you are my hope and you are my future. Lord, forgive me for the times I did not seek your Godly counsel. Father, I realize that you know what is best for me. Lord, I desire your will to be my will. Oh God! I need you every minute of every day to strengthen me where I am weak. Lord, there are promises that have not manifested yet, but I know you are God and you cannot lie; they will come to pass. Lord, I thank you for what my eyes have seen and what my ears have heard. Lord I thank you for the many blessings you have bestowed upon me. Father, I need you to hold me in the hollow of your loving hands. These precious blessings, I ask in your holy name. Amen.

Chapter 2

CRUSHED, BUT STILL STANDING

On September 17, 1989, South Carolina was hit by Hurricane Hugo; a year I will never forget. I remember listening to the news that day as the meteorologist was advising people to vacate their homes especially if they occupied a mobile home. My family had strongly advised me to vacate because they feared for the safety of my children and me. However, I was determined to stay home. We lost our home and all our contents. We were homeless and I was devastated. During the storm the roof was blown off our home. We felt the rain fall on us like drenching fury showers. We now had to run for cover and travel to safety in the midst of the horrible storm called Hugo. What a powerful God. Although our home was badly damaged, My Father protected our lives from destruction during the storm. You can be stripped down to nothing so that your own power and arrogance can be recognized. God deserves the glory and honor due His name for HIS power. Some things we bring on ourselves and some things God will allow to happen in order for the Glory to be His and His alone. ***Proverbs 16:18 (NKJV)*** *Pride goeth before destruction, and an haughty spirit before a fall.* I am learning that we can listen to what someone is saying to us and not even hear them. There is a price to pay for not listening. God has given all of His children the ability to hear; however we must be willing to obey Him when He speaks. God's Word is full of WARNING for His people if we would only heed.

Every Christian virtually passes through two phases in his search of humility. In the first stage, he fears and flies and pursues deliverance from all that can humble him. He prays for humility, at times very sincerely; but in his secret heart, he prays more, if not in word, then in demand, to be kept from the very things that will make him humble. Humility is at the heart of Christ-likeness. We follow the one who "made himself nothing." ***James 4:6 (NKJV)*** *God opposes the proud but shows favor to the humble.* We must always remember that we were created by the only perfect one, our "Lord and Savior, Jesus Christ." We must know that without the Lord and His anointing, we are nothing and can do nothing. All that we are or ever hope to become is in the hands of all mighty God. We should admit, we are not good at everything. We can only walk in our own calling and recognize our own faults and be accountable for our actions. We judge others because it's easier than looking at ourselves. When we judge others, it causes strife in our relationships, and judging others prevents new relationships from forming. It hinders us from seeking to improve ourselves and seeking help from the Holy Spirit. Everyone wants to be humble; nobody wants to be humbled.

God speaks to us in different ways. However most of the time, God speaks to me through His Word or He brings confirmation from someone that I trust. I was sitting in church sometime back and my pastor was preaching on the topic of forgiveness. "He stated that when we don't forgive others, God will not forgive us. Also, he stated that when we do not forgive that God's anointing will not be on our lives." My desire is to possess all that the good Lord has for me. I believe that arrogance and pride have a lot to do with unforgiveness. As I sat there, I began to pray in my spirit asking the Lord to forgive me for any un-forgiveness that I may have against anyone, knowing or unaware.

Luke 18:9-14 (NKJV), *⁹Also He spoke this parable to some who trusted in themselves that they were righteous, and despised others: ¹⁰Two men went up to the temple to pray, one a Pharisee and the other a tax collector. ¹¹The Pharisee stood and prayed thus with himself, 'God, I thank you that I am not like other men—extortioners, unjust, adulterers, or even as this tax collector. ¹²I fast twice a week; I give tithes of all that I possess. ¹³And the tax collector, standing afar off, would not so much as raise his eyes to heaven, but beat his breast, saying, 'God, be merciful to me a sinner!' ¹⁴I tell you, this man went down to his house justified rather than the other; for everyone who exalts himself will be humbled, and he who humbles himself will be exalted."* We should learn to listen more than we talk.

❋ PRAYER ❋
✻✻✻✻✻

Oh Father, in the mighty name of Jesus, thank you for this day. Lord, I thank you for your goodness and your grace. Lord, thank you for seeing what I will be with the help and guidance of your hand and your Holy Spirit. Lord, there are days that are challenging and seem unbearable for me, but Lord I know with you on my side, I have nothing to fear. Lord, my desire is to serve others, not to be served. Lord use me as you see fit. I realize that warning come before destruction. Lord, you can reach the hardest heart and you can stop the raging sea in my life. Lord where there is sadness, you can replace with happiness. Where there is confusion, you can put in peace. Lord in you there is life in abundance. Thank you Lord for being a loving and caring Father. These precious blessings, I ask in your mighty name. Amen

MY FATHER IS FAITHFUL

Psalm 91:1 (NKJV) *He who dwells in the secret place of the Most High Shall abide under the shadow of the Almighty. I will say of the LORD, He is my refuge and my fortress; My God, in Him I will trust.* I am so thankful to God and more aware of His presence and His goodness than ever before. Recently, as I was sitting at my desk working I begin to experience a feeling of discomfort. I became disoriented and weak so I laid my head down on my desk for a few minutes, thinking the feeling would pass. I began to feel worse. My coworker came over to check on me and immediately called the nurse. I was told I looked tired and drained. My blood pressure was very, very low. At that moment, I was unable to stand. However I was alert enough to call on the name of Jesus to myself. Shortly afterwards, I left work and went to see my physician. When I arrived at his office, he sent me directly to the hospital; upon arrival, I was treated as a stroke patient. During all of this, I was very concerned, but not worried; because, I knew my God would take care of me. I still have work to do for Him and His kingdom. ***Philippians 4:6-8 (NKJV)*** *⁶Be anxious for nothing, but in everything by prayer and supplication, with thanksgiving, let your requests be made known to God; ⁷and the peace of God, which surpasses all understanding, will guard your hearts and minds through Christ Jesus. 8Finally, brethren, whatever things are true, whatever things are noble, whatever things are just, whatever things are pure, whatever things are lovely, whatever things are of good report, if there is any virtue and if there is anything praiseworthy—meditate on these things."*

The ER physician ran a battery of tests, and they all came back negative. The admitting physicians ruled out my having a stroke and said I was pre-diabetic. What an awesome Father we serve. There are some things in this life for which we have no explanation, but one thing is certain, God will take care of His children. I am more determined than ever to live my life with more zeal for the Lord than ever before. What the devil meant for my bad, God turned around for my good. I said to the devil, "you should have killed me when you had a chance, look out because I am back!" ***Psalm 91:9-11 (NKJV)*** *⁹Because you have made the LORD, who is my refuge, Even the Most High, your dwelling place, ¹⁰No evil shall befall you, Nor shall any plague come near your dwelling; ¹¹For He shall give His angels charge over you, To keep you in all your ways.* Consigning ourselves to His protection and pledging our daily devotion to Him will keep us safe in the arms of The Almighty. We have angels that are assigned to us. One of the functions of angels is to watch over believers. I do not believe anything in life happens by chance.

Psalm 34:1 (NKJV) *I will bless the LORD at all times: His praise shall continually be in my mouth.* During my short stay in the hospital, I continued to have praise for my God on the inside; praise is what I do. Praise should be a life style, not just exercised when it is convenient. Our God deserves to be praised. When we praise God, praise ushers us into the presence of our God. Realizing that life is short and tomorrow is not promised helps us to use the time that we have more wisely and for eternal good. Because God has given us the desire for eternal life, we should not be satisfied with merely existing, but our goal should be living our lives to the fullest. Our desire should be to see God's eternal plan revealed in our lives. ***Psalm 32:7 (KJV)*** *Thou art my hiding place; thou shalt preserve me* *from trouble; thou shalt compass me about with songs of deliverance.*

Psalm 33:4 (KJV) *For the word of the LORD is right; and all his works are done in truth.* When all my test results came back negative, God showed me His awesomeness. He cannot lie. All God's words are true and trustworthy. The Bible is reliable, because unlike people, God does not lie, change his words, or leave His promises unfulfilled. We can trust the Bible because it contains the words of a Holy, trustworthy, and unchangeable God. God promises great blessing to His people, but many of these blessings require our active participation. He will free us from fear, deliver us from trouble, guard us, show us kindness, supply our needs, listen to us when we talk to Him, and redeem us. However, we must do our part. We can appropriate His blessings when we seek Him, and cry out to Him. **Psalm 37: 1-3 (KJV)** *¹Fret not thyself because of evildoers, neither be thou envious against the workers of iniquity. ²For they shall soon be cut down like the grass, and wither as the green herb. ³Trust in the LORD, and do good; so shalt thou dwell in the land, and verily thou shalt be fed.* We have nothing to fear, but fear itself.

PRAYER

Gracious and Everlasting Father, thank you for another opportunity to praise your Holy and righteous name. Lord, you keep on showing your goodness, your mercy, and your unwavering love to me. Lord, thank you for being so good to me and my family. Lord, you are an ever-present help in my time of need. Father, I am honored and delighted to call you my Father, my friend. Indeed, you are everything to me. Lord, it is such an awesome privilege to be your child. Lord, you keep on looking out for me. your goodness and your protection are endless. Lord, your faithfulness is everlasting. Thank you Jesus. Lord, continue to hold me close. Lord, I love you, and adore you. In Jesus name Amen.

CLAIM YOUR INHERITANCE

As children of the most High King, we are the seed of Abraham! That means everything God promised Abraham belongs to you. It has been passed down to you through Jesus. Abraham's blessing is your inheritance! The Word of God has willed the blessing to you. **Genesis 12:1-2 (HCSB)** *¹Go out from your land, your relatives, and your father's house to the land that I will show you. I will make you into a great nation. ²I will bless you, I will make your name great, and you will be a blessing.* We are to bless others and God will bless us in the process. My father had a saying, "With a tight fist, nothing can get out and nothing can come in." It was THE BLESSING of GOD that made Abraham rich! God's blessing caused him to prosper wherever he went.

Genesis 13:2 (HCSB) *Abram was very rich in livestock, silver and gold. Now Lot, who was traveling with Abram, also had flocks, herds, and tents. But the land was unable to support them as long as they stayed together, for they had so many possessions that they could not stay together.* When God blesses He really blesses and everyone takes notice.

Webster's dictionary defines the word "bless" as to cause to prosper, to make happy, to bestow favor upon, to consecrate to holy purposes, to make successful, to make prosperous in temporal concerns pertaining to this life, to guard and preserve. Notice that Abraham wasn't greedy or concerned about his own welfare. He had a covenant of blessing with God and he knew God would bring him success no matter where he lived. ***Genesis 15:1 (Holman Christian Standard Bible)*** *After these events, the word of the Lord came to Abram in a vision: Do not be afraid, Abram. I am your shield; your reward will be great."*

We should take that promise and put our name in it. After all, it's ours! We are the seed of Abraham. I made the decision to take God at His Word; I was faced with debt and poor credit because of poor choices in my past. God gave me a plan to rebuild my credit and pay off my debt. I am almost there, thanks be to God! God is not going to do for us what He has given us the ability to do for ourselves. Our credit and reputation is very important to God. He has been as faithful to me as He was to Abraham! God keeps His promises.

Genesis 17:6-7 (KJV) *⁶And I will make thee exceeding fruitful, and I will make nations of thee, and kings shall come out of thee. ⁷And I will establish my covenant between me and thee and thy seed after thee in their generations for an everlasting covenant, to be a God unto thee, and to thy seed after thee.*

The true blessing of Abraham will enable you to prosper no matter what is happening around you. It will cause you to increase in the midst of recessions, depressions and every other kind of economic calamity the devil can dream up. Our Father is not a Father of lack or shortage. We are not dependent on the economic cycles of this natural realm. You're not dependent on what the Federal Government does. We are dependent on our covenant with The Almighty God and that never changes! God's Word never changes and is not dependent on our situations or circumstances. God said we are "blessed," and so be it. The company that you are employed with is blessed just because you're there.

Genesis chapter 41 (KJV) speaks of Abraham's great-grandson, Joseph, started out as a slave in the ungodly nation of Egypt. But because he was the seed of Abraham, he ended up saving that nation from being destroyed by famine. Not only that, he became the most powerful man in the nation next to Pharaoh himself. The entire country was blessed because of Joseph and his covenant with God! **Romans 15:4 (AKJV)** *For whatsoever things were written aforetime were written for our learning, that we through patience and comfort of the scriptures might have hope.* I challenge you to meditate on God's word for strength, direction, and so much more.

PRAYER
✸✸✸✸✸

Oh God, thank you for your loving kindness. Father, I thank you for being so good and merciful to me. Lord, this is a new day with another opportunity to lift your Holy and righteous name. Father, your strength is renewing me every day. Thank you for seeing me as I am going to be and not as I am. Lord, you look beyond my faults and see my need. Thank you, Lord, for your unconditional love for me. Lord, bless everyone reading this book. Help them to lean and depend on you. Help them to realize they are the inheritance of Abraham. Lord, what you promised Abraham, also applies to us. In Jesus' mighty name, we pray all these things. Amen.

I REACHED A TURNING POINT

At age 17, I was united in Holy matrimony to a man that made my life miserable. First, let me share, I was not saved. I did not know the importance of consulting God about anything. I was broken, seeking love in all the wrong places and in other people. Broken people attract broken people. I thought he was the man of my dreams; little did I know he would cause me much pain and heartache. However, all was not lost; out of that marriage, God blessed us with a beautiful daughter. When we choose to leave God out of our plans, we are headed for disaster. I was often abused verbally and physically and my self-esteem was very low. I did not believe that God cared or loved me because of my inner pain and struggle. Looking back on those years of pain, I also realize my husband was also hurting and had unresolved issues himself. Hurting people hurt other people, especially people that are close to them. I am not in any way minimizing how much he hurt me; however, God revealed to me the hurt and pain that he inflected upon me, he was also experiencing within himself.

I often wondered, "where is God, and how could He allow me to go through so much pain?" I believe that experience was a major turning point in my life. I was in so much pain and agony, had tried other things, but received no comfort or direction. I turned to God for comfort. I am not certain if I believed He would comfort me, but I knew God was my last resort because I had nowhere else to turn. The world as I knew it was dark and very cold. The people that I trusted the most let me down. What a mighty God we serve! I know now that God saw through my tears, my pain, and my fears. ***Psalm 23:1-4 (KJV)*** *a Psalm of David The LORD is my shepherd; I shall not want.*

He maketh me to lie down in green pastures: he leadeth me beside the still waters. He restoreth my soul: he leadeth me in the paths of righteousness for his name's sake. Yea, though I walk through the valley of the shadow of death, I will fear no evil: for thou art with me; thy rod and thy staff they comfort me.

I remember a friend came over for a visit and my husband went to the door and told her I was not home. I was so afraid of him that I stayed quiet until she left. I was a prisoner in my home. A part of me thought that was love; maybe my husband loved me so much that he did not want to share me with anyone else. When we do not know our worth or the love that God has for us, we accept counterfeit love or any carbon copy of love and affection. Thank God that today, I know the love of my Heavenly Father. We tend to settle for much less than God's best for us when we do not know who we are in Christ. Thank God for His unconditional love. **Psalm 91:1-2,** *(HCSB)* *¹The one who lives under the protection of the Most High dwells in the shadow of the Almighty. ²I will say to the Lord, "My refuge and my fortress, my God, in whom I trust."*

I am so thankful for God's mercy and His awesome grace that He gives me daily. What a wonderful Father and friend we have in Jesus. God is amazing. I love the Lord with all my heart and soul. My greatest desire is to please Him. When I think back on my life, how far God has brought me, and the things He has delivered me from, my soul cries out, "Thank you, Jesus, for saving me! At times, I miss the mark. I do wrong and have thoughts that are contrary to God, but He loves me still. **Jeremiah 1:5 (HCSB)** *I chose you before I formed you in the womb; I set you apart before you were born. I appointed you a prophet to the nations.* Trouble and hard times will lead you either to God, or away from God. Life and circumstances will beat the life out of you if you do not know who your Father is and hide His word within your heart. I realize that life is a series of events, some good and some not so good, but through it all, everything works together for our good. By no means am I saying abuse of any kind is acceptable; however, what I am saying is that God and the Holy Spirit will use your misfortunes to bless others. **Psalm 91: 4 (HCSB)** *He will cover with His feathers; you will take refuge under His wings. His faithfulness will be a protective shield.* God is faithful and because God is always with me, I am never alone. Although there are many days and nights that you may feel alone and lonely, I want to encourage you to never settle for less than God's best for you.

PRAYER

Thank you Jesus!! Every day God sees me as His child, a work in progress. I am so thankful for the favor of God on my life. I am so thankful that He loves me the way I am. I do not have to pretend to be someone else. I wore a mask for too long and I hid the real me for too long. Thank you Lord for allowing me to walk in my calling that you ordained. I realize my God paid an ultimate price for my freedom and liberty. I am so appreciative to the Lord for all of His daily benefits. I love the Lord for who He is to me. I love the Lord, because He first loved me. Lord, cause me to seek you first and your plan for my life. Father, you are so awesome to me. Lord, I love you and honor you. All these blessings I ask in Jesus' mighty name. Amen.

A HEART ISSUE

When I first came to Christ, I would often hear others talk about hearing from God. My desire was to hear God speak to me. I was under the false assumption at that time that God only spoke to a select group of people, and I was not part of that group. Through studying God's word and getting His revelation, I have learned better. God does speak, in a clear and audible voice, He does not yell or scream. Oh yes, I know His voice and can hear him clearly. I believe our hearts have to be conditioned to hear clearly from the Lord.

Before we had caller ID on our telephones when my family members called me, I knew their voice instantly because we spent a lot of time together. Our God is no different, when you spend quality time with Him, you get to know His voice. According to ***John 10:27 (NKJV)*** *My sheep hear My voice, and I know them, and they follow Me.*

I find it ironic that, we, as Christians can hear from God regarding some things and we are unable to hear Him in others. Most of the time, God speaks to me through His written Word; however, there have been other times, I will get confirmation from other people. My Pastor preached a message on hearing from God. God speaks clearly, and very concisely. Some of the points he made were: God can speak to anyone because we are His followers. The problem is not God's ability to speak, but our ability to hear Him. The problem is never God…it is always us. We must condition ourselves to hear from God by getting in His presence and being obedient to His word.

John 10:3-5 (NKJV) *³To him the doorkeeper opens, and the sheep hear his voice; and he calls his own sheep by name and leads them out. ⁴And when he brings out his own sheep, he goes before them; and the sheep* *follow him, for they know his voice. ⁵Yet they will by no means follow a stranger, but will flee from him, for they do not know the voice of strangers."*

Would you open your door to a stranger? To some of you God may be a stranger, but there is a remedy, accept Him into your heart and live the life He has planned for you. So many people rob themselves of the intimacy that they could have with our awesome Father.

I believe one of the things that stops us from hearing from God is our own stubbornness. When we refuse to follow His amazing word. Hearing from God is easy…He does not stutter nor does He scream. God is a gentleman and He is an awesome communicator. Spend time in His word; getting to know Him, learn His ways and His character, He longs to hear from you. When we get serious with God, God will get serious with us. According to **Ephesians 5:5 (KJV)** *For this ye know, that no whoremonger, nor unclean person, nor covetous man, who is an idolater, hath any inheritance in the kingdom of Christ and of God.*

God wants closeness with us and to communicate with us, however it is a two-way communication. This is manifested in our relationship with God. God talks, we listen. We talk, God listens. God loves us so much that He sent Jesus to take our place on the old rugged cross. *Jeremiah 29:11-13 (NIV) ¹¹For I know the plans I have for you, declares the Lord, plans to prosper you and not to harm you, plans to give you hope and a future. ¹²Then you will call on me and come and pray to me, and I will listen to you. ¹³you will seek me and find me when you seek me with all your heart."* God had the perfect plan for our lives even before we entered into our mother's womb. I hunger and thirst for God and want to be closer to Him.

PRAYER

Lord thank you for this day, thank you for your unconditional love. Father God, in the precious name of Jesus, I thank you for your daily benefits, your awesome kindness to me. Lord, continue to draw our hearts toward you and your will. Lord, your word is our manual to follow in order for us to live a life that is pleasing to you. Lord, I long to be closer to you, I look forward to our time together. Father I realize you paid the ultimate price for me. Lord, it is easy to hear from you, when we spend time in your presence. Lord, help us to read your Word more and follow your example for our lives. Lord, we know we can lean and depend on you and your Word. Lord, help us to become sensitive to your voice. Lord, you long to have an intimate relationship with your children. Lord, forgive me for those times I put other things ahead of you. Lord you are my everything. Lord, I am so grateful for the opportunity to praise and uplift your Holy and righteous name. Thank you for being an awesome Father and friend to your undeserving children. These blessing we ask in your name, Amen.

CHAPTER 3

DISCONNECT TO CONNECT

Sometime ago I went out to start my car but it was slow to start, after a few minutes it cranked up. This happened on several occasions but on this particular day, it refused to start. I had been given several warnings, which I ignored. My mechanic said the battery had a dead cell and therefore my vehicle would not crank. A car battery contains many cells, when one cell does not work properly it can cause things within other parts of the car not to function. Our lives are similar. Sin interferes with our communication to our Heavenly Father. Sometimes, we get complacent in our sin and do not pay attention to the nudging of the Holy Spirit when He tries to get our attention.

When we admit our sin to God and ask for His forgiveness, He throws our sins into the sea of forgetfulness and remembers it no more. That does not mean we are free to do as we choose because God is willing to forgive us. ***Proverbs 3:5-6 (HCSB)*** *Trust in the Lord with all your heart, and do not rely on your own understanding; think about Him in all your ways, and He will guide you on the right paths.* Our God is a loving God and He is a God of compassion. Our God is a God of integrity, but He also chastises those whom He loves. God loves all of His children and therefore no one is exempt from His correction.

Nothing we do will ever surprise God, He is faithful and just to forgive us of our sins, when we come to Him. When God forgives us, He releases us from our sin. Sometimes, we hold on to the very things God has forgiven us for; such as bitterness, guilt, forgiveness, condemnation, and pain. We must forgive ourselves in order to be free. According to God's wise plan we can call upon Him in confidence and He will answer. God can be sought and found when we seek Him urgently and wholeheartedly. We should seek God to find the root of our problems and ask Him to help us. ***Jeremiah 29:13 (HCSB)*** *you will seek Me, and find Me, when you search for Me with all your heart.*

Hebrews 6:17-18 (HCSB) *17Because God wanted to show His unchangeable purpose even more clearly to the heirs of the promise, He guaranteed it with an oath, so that through two unchangeable things, in which it is impossible for God to lie, we who have fled for refuge might have strong encouragement to seize the hope set before us.* When we confess or admit our sins to God, He is faithful and just to forgive us. God is faithful and He cannot lie. God's word is true.

Jeremiah 29: 11-12 (HCSB) 11For I know the plans, I have for you—this is the Lord's declaration – plans for your welfare, not for disaster, to give you a future and a hope. 1You will call on Me and come and pray to Me, and I will listen to you. Lord, I thank you for limitless mercy and unending grace. God does not hold grudges nor does God hold our past sins against us. God created us, He knows we will sin and miss the mark but He is there to help us. It does not matter what we have done, our Father is willing to forgive us. Our thoughts are not God's thoughts; He is just and too wise to make mistakes. Never be deceived by man, read God's word for yourself and ask Him for His revelation, He will reveal His word to you. I believe God's greatest desire is for His children to trust Him. We must get outside the boat and have some walk on water faith.

PRAYER

Thank you, Father for this peaceful day. Thank you, Lord for your goodness and your mercy that you have bestowed upon me. Lord, you are a wonderful God, in spite of my faults and imperfections. Lord, I am a work in progress; I thank you for not giving up on me. Father, I thank you for loving me, and taking excellent care of me. Lord, make me more like you, create in me a pure heart and renew a right spirit within me. Teach me, oh Lord, how to pray and what to pray for. Father, mold me and make me into your image. Lord, let my light shine that others will see you in me. Lord, I am very thankful to be your child, and to call you Father. Lord, when life gets confusing the tears flow and sadness arise, I know I can lean on you. Lord, challenges will come but I know in you I have a hiding place within your loving arms. Lord, give me the strength I need to endure the trials that life will bring. Father, heal the sick, and wrap your loving arms around the bereaved families everywhere. Lord, strengthen the weak, and give your peace to the confused minds of your children. These blessings we ask in your mighty name, Amen.

RIGHT THINKING PRODUCES, RIGHT BEHAVIOR

Have you ever felt depressed, agitated, or frustrated and did not know why? I used to stay that way, however those days are gone. I am not saying the enemy does not attempt to attack my mind, but I have learned with the help of God to replace negative thoughts with positive thoughts. Not just positive thoughts, but the Word of God; it is the final authority. I have confidence in God and confidence in myself. God wants His children to be confident, but not arrogant. We can always be confident in God. I once had a problem making eye contact with people, especially individuals whom I perceived to be more intelligent than me. I had to change my mind-set; I am learning to say what God says about me. With the help of the Holy Spirit, I no longer have that problem. ***Joshua 1:9 (HCSB)*** *Haven't I commanded you: be strong and courageous? Do not be afraid or discouraged, for the LORD your God is with you wherever you go.*

I am the righteousness of God in Christ; therefore I can produce right behavior! With the help of my Father, I can do all things. Jesus died in order for His children to live more abundantly. We must spend quality time in God's word in order to understand the Love of our Heavenly Father. In God, we never have to be in fear of what lies ahead. We all had a past, but we all have a bright future in God. When we take our minds off God, we get anxious about tomorrow and what may or may not happen, however when we focus our thoughts of God and his word, he gives us peace beyond human understanding.

Ephesians 6:10-14 (NKJV) *¹⁰Finally, my brethren, be strong in* *the Lord and in the power of His might. ¹¹Put on the whole armor of God, that you may be able to stand against the wiles of the devil. ¹²For we do not wrestle against flesh and blood, but against principalities, against powers, against the rulers of the darkness of this age, against spiritual hosts of wickedness in the heavenly places. ¹³Therefore take up the whole armor of God that you may be able to withstand in the evil day, and having done all, to stand. ¹⁴Stand therefore, having girded your waist with truth, having put on the breastplate of righteousness.*

It is imperative that we seek God daily and spend time in His word. Tough times will come and we will need to know God's word and have His word in our hearts to face various trials and the attack of the enemy.

When we are thinking on the thoughts of our Heavenly Father, our behavior will line up with our thoughts. When we meditate on the word of God, our words will be in agreement with the word of God. We make choices every day; we decide what we keep and what we throw away. ***Isaiah 55:8-9 (NLT)***

PRAYER
✶✶✶✶✶

Father, thank you, for your everlasting grace. Thank you Lord, for giving me the mind and desire to serve you. Thank you Lord, for loving me unconditionally. Lord, thank you for your peace and confidence. Lord, thank you for the gift of the Holy Spirit as my teacher and guide. Lord, thank you for your unconditional love and your daily forgiveness. Lord, help me to be bold for you. Lord, teach me your way and order my every step. Lord, where there is shame give me pride, where is doubt give me trust. Lord, where there is confusion, give me peace and clarity. Lord, help me to love like you love and help me have compassion for others, as I desire others to have for me. Lord, I am what your word says I am. Your word says I am beautifully and wonderfully made." These precious blessings I ask in your name, Amen.

SWEET REVELATION

When I was a child, I thought Easter was a special day because my parents bought my siblings and me new clothes, an Easter basket, and we looked for hidden colored eggs. Now that I am an adult and realize the true meaning of Easter, it saddens me that some children are missing out on the true meaning of the Holiday. God's resurrection is the true meaning of the celebration. Although I went to church on Easter, I did not understand the meaning of the celebration until I became of age. Children understand more than we as adults may think. I encourage you to share the true meaning of Easter with your children in their language. No child is too young to learn about the love of God. ***Proverbs 22:6 (NKJV)*** *Train up a child in the way he should go, And when he is old he will not depart from it.*

What an awesome God we serve. Celebrating Jesus and the resurrection is a wonderful experience. It is so refreshing to have the freedom and liberty to praise our Heavenly Father. When I think about our Jesus, the Lord dying on the cross for a sinner like me, I love him all the more, with all my being. ***Psalm 28:6 – 7 (NKJV)*** *⁶Blessed be the Lord, because He has heard the voice of my supplications! ⁷The Lord is my strength and my shield; My heart trusted in Him, and I am helped; Therefore my heart greatly rejoices, And with my song I will praise Him."*

Jesus made the conscious decision, without a second thought and with no regret, to die for you and me. The Lord was stretched wide and hung on an old rugged cross. He was spat on, ridiculed, and called everything but who He is. Even on the cross He was advocating for His children, He was thinking of us. God knew we would need a savior and we could not make it without Him. ***Jeremiah 31:3 (NIV)*** *The Lord appeared to us in the past, saying:" I have loved you with an everlasting love; I have drawn you* *with unfailing kindness.* It doesn't matter how far you try to run from Him, He loves you and wants to forgive you where you've gone wrong. He created you and cares about you. God, in His Love towards His children, wants so much for us to lean and depend on Him. God longs to be a part of our daily lives, He wants to bless us beyond what we can ever imagine. John 10:10 (NIV) says, "The thief comes only to steal and kill and destroy; I have come that they may have life, and have it to the full."

We have all thought, said, or done bad things the Bible calls sin. **Romans 3:23-24 (KJV)** *[23]For all have sinned, and come short of the glory of God; [24]Being justified freely by his grace through the redemption that is in Christ Jesus."* Our God is a forgiving God. He does not keep a score board of our wrongs to punish or condemn us. **Romans 5:8 (NIV)** *But God demonstrates His own love for us in this: While we were still sinners, Christ died for us.* We can't earn salvation; we are saved by God's grace when we have faith in His Son, Jesus Christ. All you have to do is believe you are a sinner, acknowledge that Christ died for your sins, and ask His forgiveness. He knows you and loves you. What matters to Him is the attitude of your heart, your honesty.

❈(PRAYER)❈
✸✸✸✸✸✸

Thank you Lord, for dying on the cross to save a sinner like me. Lord, thank you for your love, grace, and mercy. Lord, you are so wonderful and loving to your children. Lord, we adore you, and honor you. God, when I think of you hanging on that old rugged cross, beaten, spat on, and called everything that you are not, my soul cries out, "Thank you Lord, for saving me!" Jesus died in our place so we could live with Him in eternity. "Lord, we want to please you, in every way. Lord, help us to be reminded daily of your ultimate sacrifice on the cross. Lord, bless everyone reading this book; help them to share your love with others, and to honor you and the price you paid for our sins. Humbly we ask these blessings, in your precious name, Amen.

I OWN MY FAITH

I heard at an early age, "faith comes by hearing and hearing by the word of God." As a child I thought God only made Himself available to certain people, and for others He hid himself. Now as an adult, I know that God is not playing hide-and-seek…He is not elusive. Jesus is not the one who is hiding. God is not a fugitive. Some people seek after the benefits that only God can give them. The sin of fallen man is this: Man seeks the benefits of God while fleeing from God Himself. We are, by nature, fugitives. The Bible tells us repeatedly to seek after God. ***Isaiah 55:6 (KJV)*** *Seek ye the LORD while he may be found, call ye upon him while he is near:*
Hebrews 11:1 (KJV) *Now faith is the substance of things hoped for, the evidence of things not seen. For by it the elders obtained a good report.*

Without faith no man can please God. Are you seeking the benefits that you can attain from God or are you simply seeking God alone? On those days when we doubt our strength, we can ask God for His strength to persevere. On those days when we feel like the least-liked person in our homes, on our jobs, or even in our church, we can ask for confidence to stand strong in our beliefs. ***Matthew 7:7-11 (KJV)*** *⁷Ask, and it shall be given you; seek, and ye shall find; knock, and it shall be opened unto you: ⁸For every one that asketh receiveth; and he that seeketh findeth; and to him that knocketh it shall be opened. ⁹Or what man is there of you, whom if his son ask bread, will he give him a stone? ¹⁰Or if he ask a fish, will he give him a serpent? ¹¹If ye then, being evil, know how to give good gifts unto your* *children, how much more shall your Father which is in heaven give good things to them that ask him?*

In ***Ephesians 2:8-10 (KJV)*** Paul says, *⁸For by grace are ye saved through faith; and that not of yourselves: it is the gift of God: ⁹Not of works, lest any man should boast. ¹⁰For we are his workmanship, created in Christ Jesus unto good works, which God hath before ordained that we should walk in them.*

Titus. 2:11-14 (NIV) *¹¹For the grace of God has appeared that offers salvation to all people. ¹²It teaches us to say "No" to ungodliness and worldly passions, and to live self-controlled, upright and godly lives in this present age, ¹³while we wait for the blessed hope – the appearing of the glory of our great God and Savior, Jesus Christ, ¹⁴who gave himself for us to redeem us from all wickedness and to purify for himself a people that are his very own, eager to do what is good.*

Revelation 3:20-22 (KJV) ²⁰Behold, I stand at the door, and knock: if any man hear my voice, and open the door, I will come in to him, and will sup with him, and he with me. ²¹ To him that overcometh will I grant to sit with me in my throne, even as I also overcame, and am set down with my Father in his throne. ²²He that hath an ear, let him hear what the Spirit saith unto the churches. We are not waiting on God. God is waiting on us. God is not distant, or in a faraway place, He is just a prayer away. It gives our Father pleasure when his children come to Him. When my children were small and they wanted something from me, they would ask repeatedly, being very persistent until I answered their request. God is knocking on the door of your heart. Sometimes, they would hold on to the tail of my dress until I either acknowledged their presence or gave them what they wanted. We need to be persistent when we desire something from the Lord. Hold firm to his word and do not let it go until we get an answer. He is waiting…just answer the door and allow Him to enter.

PRAYER

Father thank you for this wonderful day. Thank you oh heavenly father for another opportunity to praise your Holy and righteous name. Jesus, strengthen me to persevere until my prayers are answered. Lord, help me in areas of my unbelief. Lord, I know faith without works is dead, and without faith, it is impossible to please you. Let me not waiver, but stand firm in faith. Lord help me be confident by believing, that every man is given a measure of faith. We can only acknowledge something that we already have. We already have the faith of God, and it will begin to work when we acknowledge this. Father help me to acknowledge, the faith I have on the inside of me, in Jesus' name, Amen.

A GODLY MOTHER IS A GIFT FROM GOD

Years ago I was a student at Florence Darlington Technical College. I attend a lecture, the well-known motivational speaker Dr. Ben Carson was our guest. He is the author of Gifted Hands. Doctor Carson shared that he was reared by a single mother. He talked about walking to school with card board in the bottom of his shoes. He made sure we knew he was poor. He also shared that his mother was a women of faith and prayer. She had only a 3rd grade education, but she instilled in him and his brother the importance of getting a proper education. His mother challenged them to read two books a week from the local library and write book reports. She was very innovative as she never let on that she couldn't read. The pretense of his mother inability was uncovered when he got older. How powerful is our God to hold his interest in something that his mother stood for, even though she could not accomplish the reading, she saw the bigger picture, a greater hope, a greater future. This is the power and the prayer of a Godly mother! ***Proverbs 31:28 (NKJV)*** *Her children rise up and call her blessed; her husband also, and he praises her.*

    Proverbs 1:8 (KJV) *My son, hear the instruction of thy father, and forsake not the law of thy mother.* One of the things I remember most about my mother is the love she had for her church. My mother sung in the choir, and worked in other capacities in the church. My mother prepared dinner especially Sunday's as if she was cooking for the entire community and invited her pastor and the deacons. My mother would feed people she did not know, if they needed a hot meal. She demonstrated to me her love for others by her actions. Faith without works is dead. We inherit more from our mothers than we sometimes think. My daughter said to me on numerous occasions that certain things she does, it is because she learned it from me.

    Proverbs 31: 15-18 (AMP) *[15]She rises while it is yet night and gets [spiritual] food for her household and assigns her maids their tasks. [16]She considers a [new] field before she buys or accepts it expanding prudently and not courting neglect of her present duties by assuming other duties]; with her savings [of time and strength] she plants fruitful vines in her vineyard. [17]She girds herself with strength [spiritual, mental, and physical fitness for* her God-given task] and makes her arms strong and firm. *18She tastes and sees that her gain from work [with and for God] is good; her lamp goes not out, but it burns on continually through the night [of trouble, privation, or sorrow, warning away fear, doubt, and distrust].*

She rises while it is still night and provides food for her household and portions for her servants, She evaluates a field and buys it; she plants a vineyard with her earnings. She draws on her strength and reveals that her arms are strong. She sees that her profits are good, and her lamp never goes out at night. A Godly woman speaks with wisdom and authority. She acknowledges that, God is her refuge and strength.

Proverbs 31:26-27 (NLT) *26When she speaks, her words are wise and she gives instructions with kindness.*

27She carefully watches everything in her household and suffers nothing from laziness.

I have discovered that God has given a special gift to mothers; my mother called it intuition. I believe it could also be a nudging from the Holy Spirit. A God fearing mother watches over her family. My husband says to me more times than I care to recall, "You are always putting everyone else's needs above your own." A good mother listens to God and allow Him to lead her every step. A mother realizes that God is the head of her house, and she allows Him to rule and reign. God instilled a gift within all mothers. When things are not right in the home, or with our children a good mother knows it. A God fearing mother is close to the heart of God. Mothers are slow to speak and quick to listen. A mother's prayers goes where her children goes. When the weight of the world is on their shoulders, or when they have an important decision to make, a mother is there with open arm, a shoulder to cry on, an encouraging word prayer and a pot of food to bring solace and comfort to that child. Mothers are prayer warriors, always seeking direction and answers from God. A God fearing mother is one that seek ways to make the lives of her children, and others better. A Mother's words are to heal and not bruise, and that is what the word of God does, when mothers seek His divine intervention concerning her children. Mothers allow God to be the final authority!

Matthew 12:40 (KJV) *For as Jonas was three days and three nights in the whale's belly; so shall the Son of man be three days and three nights in the heart of the earth.* As a child of God, mother, grandmother and wife, my prayer is ***Psalm 16:1-2*** *¹Preserve me, O God: for in thee do I put my trust. ²O my soul, thou hast said unto the LORD, Thou art my Lord: my goodness extendeth not to thee.*

Psalm 16:11 (KJV) *Thou wilt shew me the path of life: in thy presence is fullness of joy; at thy right hand there are pleasures for evermore.*

❧PRAYER❧
✲✲✲✲✲

Father God in the name above every name; thank you for being so good to me. Thank you for the opportunity of being a mother. I love you Lord. Father you are my all in all. You are my strength and my protector. Lord you are my rock and my shield; my fortress, and my deliverer. Thank you Lord for this wonderful day. Lord bless all mothers everywhere. Lord we realize that being a mother comes with great responsibility, but you O' Lord, have equipped all mothers with everything that we need to rear our children. Lord we thank you, we give you praise and honor, in Jesus mighty name, Amen.

CHAPTER 4

ATTRIBUTES OF A MATURE CHRISTIAN

My grandson was given a tricycle for Christmas; it had training wheels on it. When he first was given the tricycle, he was anxious to ride it, and my husband and I would push him because of his lack of balance. As time went on and the more he tried to ride his tricycle, the more independent he became. Soon, he was riding without our assistance. My husband told him recently that he would be removing the training wheels as he is now a big boy and is approaching his third birthday. However, his Papa assured him that he would not leave him alone, and he would not let him fall. I sat and watched as the training wheels were being removed, and I watched as Papa held his tricycle so he would not fall. I am so thankful that as we grow and mature into the things of God that He is always there for us and with us. **Hebrews 13:5 (NLT)** *Don't love money; be satisfied with what you have. For God has said, I will never fail you. I will never abandon you.* When we first come to the Lord and begin to understand His Word, we are considered infants in the things of the Lord, but the more we read His Word, pray, attend church and Bible study, we grow more and more in the things of God. your life should be free from the love of money. Be satisfied with what you have, for He Himself has said, "I will never leave you nor forsake you". Therefore, we may boldly say: The Lord is my helper; I will not be afraid. What can man do to me?" According to **John 16:23-24 (NLT)** ²³*At that time you won't need to ask me for* *anything. I tell you the truth, you will ask the Father directly, and he will grant your request because you use my name. ²⁴you haven't done this before. Ask, using my name, and you will receive, and you will have abundant joy.* Jesus is referring to supplication... ASKING, making a request. We should never be afraid to bring our requests to God. In fact, the Bible even tells us to do so.

In ***Philippians 4:6-7 (KJV)*** *⁶Be careful for nothing; but in everything by prayer and supplication with thanksgiving let your requests be made known unto God. ⁷And the peace of God, which passeth all understanding, shall keep your hearts and minds through Christ Jesus.* As my grandson was being pushed by his Papa, he kept saying, "Papa, do not let me fall, and all of a sudden, he stopped saying that and started smiling, because he felt secure. There is a very REAL benefit to us when we pray; in fact, have you ever noticed that when you pray about something really urgent that after you prayed, you're usually really at peace? That's because the result of our asking, or the result of our requests in prayer, will be peace of mind. Prayer is a real act of supplication.

Just as every parent in the world is delighted when they see their children growing and maturing, God is bless when He sees His children making the transition from infancy into adulthood in a spiritual sense. God wants us to move from the spiritual nursery to the spiritual battlefield. He wants us to leave the realm of milk, bibs, and diapers; He wants us to enter the realm of meat and potatoes. God's plan for every one of His children is to see them all reach spiritual maturity! He just wants us to grow up! Sad to say, a few do, some never will, and others reach for that goal daily. All of us know we are far from what we should be, but there is a genuine desire in our hearts to be all the Lord has saved us to be. Our life is filled with ups and downs with the struggles of the flesh and the spirit. We are not self-righteous, self-confident or self-reliant. We merely want to grow!

2 Timothy 2:15 (NKJ) *Study to shew thyself approved unto God, a workman that needeth not to be ashamed, rightly dividing the word of truth.*

PRAYER
✶✶✶✶✶

Oh gracious Father, thank you for your goodness and mercy. Lord we should all desire to eat solid food, which is your daily word. Thank you Lord for this day. Thank you for another opportunity to praise your mighty name. Lord help us to please you and get more understanding of your Holy Word. Help us Father to apply your Word to our daily lives and not just hearers of your awesome Word. Lord help us to mature in the things that bring you honor and glory. your Word is a lamp unto our feet. Lord help us to seek you and your will and direction for our lives. In Jesus' precious name we pray these things. Amen.

PEACE

I am honored and bless to have a Father that will never leave me nor will He forsake me. I am thankful that He answers prayer. My husband asked me for my keys to start my car before leaving for work one morning; I usually put my keys in the same place all the time. For some unknown reason I could not find my keys. I started praying Lord I need my keys, help me find my keys. As we all know time does not stop because of our emergencies. My husband and I continued to look for my car keys, however we were unsuccessful. I could feel the tension in my body building; I begin to talk to myself out loud saying, Lord it's going to be alright and this too will pass. I did not want to be late for work and have to explain why I was tardy. ***John 14:27 (ESV)*** *Peace I leave with you; my peace I give to you. Not as the world gives do I give to you. Let not your hearts be troubled, neither let them be afraid.*

Do not allow the enemy to steal your joy. Things happen but we choose how we are going to respond. I believe because of my prayer life and my connection to the Father I was able to call on God for the calmness I needed quickly and He answered me. My God is a right now God. I am so appreciative to God for loving me, protecting me, and guiding me each day. Prayer is powerful and changes the condition of our hearts. We all can pray, at anytime and anywhere. Activate your prayer life and watch the manifestation of the Holy Spirit. I am so thankful that God is always available when I call on Him. Our God can be in all places at the same time. I love the Lord because he first love me!! ***Philippians 4:6-7 (ESV)*** *6Do not be anxious about anything, but in everything by prayer and supplication with thanksgiving let your requests be made known to God. 7And the peace of God, which surpasses all understanding, will guard your hearts and your minds in Christ Jesus.*

Psalm 91:2 (KJV) *I will say of the LORD, He is my refuge and my fortress: my God; in him will I trust.* Our words have power. Out of your mouth the heart speaks, this is one of the main reasons we should spend time in God's word. Situations and circumstances can change in an instant, our frame of mind depend of how we react in emergencies.

Psalm 32:8 (Holman Christian Bible) *I will instruct you and show you the way to go; with my eye on you, I will give counsel.* When we spend time with God and in His word He will reveal things to us that otherwise we would not know. He will give us direction to prevent pit falls. Our God will tell you when to go right and when to go left and when to be still. Time with God is valuable. you are a product of what you do every day. Having a daily date with God is the best investment you will ever make. A daily date with our Lord and Savior means to get before God in prayer and reading His word. It is a time you shut out all other distractions and focus on God and God alone. It is a time to commune with God and enjoy the presence of a loving Father.

Jeremiah 33:3 (KJV) *Call unto me, and I will answer thee and show thee great and mighty things, which thou knowest not.* Quiet time enables you to gain knowledge from God about our life, needs, desires and so much more.

Have you ever gotten stuck in something and could not gain an understanding? Spending time in the presence of God, our thoughts become clearer and we get new perspective and new revelation. ***Job 12:13 (NLT)*** *But true wisdom and power are found in God; counsel and understanding are His.*

Isaiah 30:21 (KJ21) *And thine ears shall hear." a word behind thee, saying, This is the way, walk ye in it, when ye turn to the right hand, and when ye turn to the left.* When we don't know what to do, or which way to go, our God will direct us in our quiet time with Him.

❧PRAYER❧
✳✳✳✳✳✳

Thank you Lord for this day; for the many blessings you have bestowed upon me and my family. Thank you Lord for this new day that you have allow me to see. Thank you Lord for keeping me in my right mind and for watching over me all night long. Father I thank you for friends and family. Lord thank you for giving me a mind and the desire to praise your Holy and righteous name. Lord forgive me of all my sins, and all thoughts that are not of you. Oh God create in me a pure and clean heart and make me more like you. These mighty blessings I ask in your name, Amen.

GOD'S MASTERPIECE

A former colleague asked me some years ago, Mrs. Shepard have you ever considered furthering your education? My response was school? I did not think I could succeed. At that point in my life, I did not know then what I know now what my Father said about me. I am His masterpiece. **Philippians 4:13 (Holman Christian Bible)** *I am able to do all things through Him who strengthens me."* It is so important to read God's word daily, and know for yourself what the word say about you. Ask God and he will give you revelation. God will also, put the right people in your path along the way, that will help you get to where he is taking you. My colleague was very persistent, she kept encouraging me, so I applied thinking in my mind I would not be accepted. To my surprise I was accepted, because of God and his leading, I did well.

Do not tolerate negative people. Fill your life with positive people because negative people will sap the life right out of you. Believe God; take Him at His word. Our thoughts and words have power.

Isaiah 41: 10 (Holman Christian Bible) *Do not fear for I am with you; do not be afraid, for I am your God. I will strengthen you; I will help you, I will hold on to you with my righteous right hand.* God's word is true and He is faithful.

When we believe what the word of God says about us we have nothing to fear. Most of my young adult life, I feared being rejected and not accepted, but thank God today, I know who I am in Him. It is a must to know who we are in Christ Jesus. God has given us everything we need to be successful; the main ingredient is keeping God first in everything we do. Fear will paralyze us and attempt to circumvent the will of God for our lives; keep in mind fear is the opposite of faith. I have learned in most instances it is not what others say about us but, it is our own thoughts that hold us captive. We are God's masterpiece, everything he made was good. Ponder in your mind the skill it must have taken for God to create us. We are beautifully and wonderfully made, in the image of our Holy and righteous Father.

Proverbs 3:5–6 (Holman Christian Bible) *⁵Trust in the Lord with all your heart, ⁶and do not rely on your own understanding; think about Him in all your ways, and He will guide you on the right paths.*

It is imperative that we study God's word and say to ourselves what His word says about us, in order to overcome fear and doubt. We must replace negative with positive. It is the enemy's job to contradict the word of God. He wants to discourage us. The only weapon we have to fight the enemy is God's word and prayer; they are powerful tools that God has given us.

Lord help my unbelief. Help me in every area of my life. We

are not hindered by what other people say about us, we are hindered by our own hesitation, distrust and inner fears.

❈ PRAYER ❈
✾✾✾✾✾

Thank you Father God for this day. Thank you Lord for your love and divine favor on my life. Lord thank you for watching over me and my family as we slept through the night. Thank you Heavenly Father for keeping me in my right mind. Oh God how I love and adore you. Lord I realize today that nothing will happen to me today that you and I cannot handle. Father my life is not mine; it is to you I belong. Lord forgive me of my sins, and any thoughts that I have that is contrary to you. Create in me a pure and clean heart. Lord thank you for your faithfulness and love for me. Lord give me the strength I need to do your will. Lord help me to love myself and others with the love you shower me with daily. Father touch the brokenhearted, heal the sick bodies, and double mindedness of your children. Lord I stand against mental illness, worry, depression, confusion, slothfulness and stagnation. Lord you have provided all that we need to live a fruitful and productive life. Lord help your people to stand and be bold declaring your word. Lord continue to bless your people with whatever they stand in need of, in Jesus Holy and righteous name, Amen.

HEED THE CALL

I visited a Verizon phone center recently. When I entered the building, I was asked by the store representative to have a seat. I was assured that someone would assist me shortly, however, there were several people ahead of me. As I waited, I noticed there were people coming in and people going out continuously. I thought to myself, what would happen when I call on Jesus and he said have a seat, others are ahead of you, and wait your turn. We as human – being have such busy lives. Where does God fit in our schedules and our daily agendas? Take a moment, breathe slowly, and now exhale. Smell God's aroma and enjoy His fresh air. Take some time and relax, enjoy the natural things that God has given to us.

According to **Matthew 11:27** *All things are delivered to me of my Father: and no man knoweth who the Son is, but the Father; and who the Father is, but the Son, and he to whom the Son will reveal him. James 1:22(KJV) "But be doers of the word and not hearers only, deceiving yourselves."* We put so many things ahead of God. As advance as technology is, it does break down, stop working and need to be repair from time to time. Although I did not particularly like having to wait, I was determine to handle my business, so I waited because, my business was that important to me. I have heard it said, we make time to what is important to us. If that is true, where is God on your list?

Luke 10:27(KJV) *And he answering said, Thou shalt love the Lord thy God with all thy heart, and with all thy soul, and with all thy strength, and with all thy mind; and thy neighbor as thyself.* God is never busy. God would never say, "Someone is ahead of you, wait your turn;" I will be with you shortly. Think back to a time, when you got so busy during your day, that you never consult God about your plans for that day, nor did you ask God's opinion about that important decision you had to make. God still gives us favor, and supplies all our needs. God still answers our prayers when we take time to pray, even though He is the last person on our list some days.

Jeremiah 33:3 (KJV) *Call unto me, and I will answer thee, and* *shew thee great and mighty things, which thou knowest not.* We are moving at such fast pace, wanting to get things done, that we forget, if it was not for God, His love and compassion, we would cease to exist. Our God always has time for His creation. He is never too busy. We have a direct line to Heaven through prayer. A thought to ponder: how often do you take advantage of that free gift?

Psalm 141: 2, (NLT) *Accept my prayer as incense offered to you, and my upraised hands as an evening offering.* I was having a conversation with a good friend of mine, and she stated "everywhere she goes; her cell phone is with her, even in the shower, because she does not want to miss a call. How many of us, listen that attentively for God's call? According to **Isaiah 55: 6 (NKJV)** *Seek the LORD while He may be found, call upon Him while He is near.*

PRAYER

Thank you Lord for this awesome day, for life, health and strength. Thank you for sending your angels to watch over my family and me as we slept through the night. Early this morning you touch me eyes and they came open. Lord where would I be without you? Lord, you are my all and all. Thank you Lord for your provision, for all that you have done in my life and all that you are going to do. Lord, you are an awesome Father, we love and adore you. Lord there have been times, when I have prayed and you seem so far from me, but deep in my heart I know you are always with me. Father help my doubt and unbelief. Lord, continue to bless us. Give us a heart of thanksgiving. Lord help us to seek the giver and not the gifts. Lord, we seek to please you, above all else. Father we love you and magnify your Holy and righteous name. Thank you Lord for loving us, and taking excellent care of us. These blessings we ask in your precious name, Amen

Chapter 5

THORNS

When I was in middle school, my struggles with mathematics became evident. The irony was I enjoyed doing math to a certain degree. Part of my struggle was the fact I did not have a solid foundation. While attending Francis Marion University (FMU), I completed my entire curriculum two semesters before I actually graduated because of my deficiency in mathematics. Mathematics was a thorn in my side. I vividly remember walking the grounds of FMU campus asking the Lord, why? Why was this subject so challenging for me?

In retrospect, I prayed more and sought God more, because he was the only one that could give me His wisdom and revelation. To this day, I am thankful for that experience. It did not feel good at that time, but it changed my life. That "thorn" taught me never to give up on my dreams. God's Word tells us "with God, all things are possible".

2 Corinthians 12:7- 9(ESV) *[7]So to keep me from becoming conceited because of the surpassing greatness of the revelations, a thorn was given me in the flesh, a messenger of Satan to harass me, to keep me from becoming conceited. [8]Three times I pleaded with the Lord about this, that it should leave me. [9]But he said to me, My grace is sufficient for you, for my power is made perfect in weakness. Therefore I will boast all the more gladly of my weaknesses, so that the power of Christ may rest upon me."*

We may never know as to why God allows us to experience the trials and tribulations in our walk with Him. I will trust God even when I do not understand His method. I believe there are some thorns we all will have to endure, but with God's grace we will come out as pure gold. We have to give God glory for what He does and not take the credit for what only He can do! Just as in Paul's case, God does not want us to become conceited and give ourselves praise, honor and glory that are due to Him. In spite of Paul's thorn, God used him mightily for the furtherance and advancement of His Gospel. The existence of illness or suffering in a believer's life does not necessarily constitute a sinful life or a life that lacks faith.

1 Peter 4:12-13(NKJV) *¹²Beloved, do not think it strange concerning the fiery trial which is to try you, as though some strange thing happened to you; ¹³but rejoice to the extent that you partake of Christ's sufferings, that when His glory is revealed, you may also be glad with exceeding joy.*

In this life we will face trials and hardships. Our God is here to help us come through them, if we only trust Him. God did not promise us that our lives would be free of pain, hurt, disappointments, and sorrow. But, what He did promise is that He will be with us, and He would never leave us alone. I want to encourage you to hold on; your blessing is on the way. If you refuse to give up and hold on to God's unchanging hand, you will succeed. I believe one of the reasons we do not see the manifestation of God's goodness is because we give up too soon. We must remember the battle is not ours to fight it is the Lord's. Father help us to spend more time with you and in your word. Lord your heart is in your perfect word.

ᛞ PRAYER ᛞ
✻✻✻✻✻

Thank you Heavenly Father for this magnificent day that's filled with your love and goodness. Thank you for your divine wisdom and devotion to your children. Thank you Lord for thorns because they keep me on bended knees. Lord, there are so many things I do not understand, but I know and trust that you know what is best for me. Lord, I do not know what thorns your children may be facing today, but I know you will bring them through. Lord heal the sick, clear up misunderstandings, guide the hearts and minds of your people. Lord help us not to worry about tomorrow but stay in the present. Lord heal the broken hearted in spirit, and Lord where there is sadness bring your joy. Lord we know that weeping may endure for a night but your joy cometh in the morning. Give us strength and courage Father, to trust you and persevere. Lord, you are an amazing Father to your children. We realize you want only the best for us. Lord our thorns keep us close to you and your will. Father in this flesh and in this world, we will never reach perfection, but we are striving to do your will daily. These humble blessings we ask in your name, Amen.

UNLOCK YOUR GOD-GIVEN POTENTIAL

When we can see the vision, our God can do the impossible. **Philippians 4:13 (NKJV)** *I can do all things through Christ that*

strengthens me. Mistakes and failures will happen, but when it does, ask God to activate the strength He has given you to bounce back. As I often say, life is a process; we are forever learning, willingly or unwillingly. Think of your journey as a long vacation. If you drive indefinitely without an oil change or without stopping for fuel, you will burn out and run out of fuel. For every right decision we make, the closer we will come to our goal. The Word of God says, *"We have not because we ask not."* We must speak life into our desires and dreams, by saying what God's Word says. If we never experience failure, we would not know what success felt like; and if we never failed at anything, how could we learn? **Proverbs 25:28(NKJV)** *Whoever has no rule over his own spirit Is like a city broken down, without walls.* Self-control is the ability to respond to the ongoing demands of experience within the range of emotions in a manner that is socially tolerable and sufficiently flexible. It is to permit spontaneous reactions, as well as the ability to delay spontaneous reactions as needed. It can also be defined as extrinsic and intrinsic processes responsible for monitoring, evaluating, and modifying emotional reactions that will help aide you in a positive direction.

Every day, we are continually exposed to a wide variety of potentially arousing positive and negative influences. Inappropriate influences can impede our progress; therefore, it is imperative that we engage daily in the Word of God.

Galatians 3:23-26 (KJV) *23But before faith came, we were kept under the law, shut up unto the faith which should afterwards be revealed. 24Wherefore the law was our schoolmaster to bring us unto Christ, that we might be justified by faith. 25But after that faith is come, we are no longer under a schoolmaster. 26For ye are all the children of God by faith in Christ Jesus.* God does not require that we control what is beyond our God given ability. Some things in life we must learn to accept peacefully, yield to, and work our way through. Despite self-control's obvious importance, we should not limit our understanding of these words to merely the stringent discipline of the individual's passions and appetites. These words also include the notions of having good sense, sober wisdom, moderation and soundness of mind as contrasted to insanity. We can do nothing on our own; we need the help of the Holy Spirit to lead and guide us from moment to moment.

1 Corinthians 12:12-25 (NIV) 12The body is a unit, though it is made up of many parts; and though all its parts are many, they form one body. So it is with Christ. 13For we were all baptized by one Spirit into one body--whether Jews or Greeks, slave or free--and we were all given the one Spirit to drink. 14Now the body is not made up of one part but of many. 15If the foot should say, "Because I am not a hand, I do not belong to the body," it would not for that reason cease to be part of the body. 16And if the ear should say, "Because I am not an eye, I do not belong to the body," it would not for that reason cease to be part of the body. 17If the whole body were an eye, where would the sense of hearing be? If the whole body were an ear, where would the sense of smell be? 18But in fact God has arranged the parts in the body, every one of them, just as he wanted them to be. 19If they were all one part, where would the body be? 20As it is, there are many parts, but one body. 21The eye cannot say to the hand, "I don't need you!" And the head cannot say to the feet, "I don't need you!" 22On the contrary, those parts of the body that seem to be weaker are indispensable, and the parts that we think are less honorable we treat with special honor. 23And the parts that are unpresentable are treated with special modesty, 24while our presentable parts need no special treatment. But God has combined the members of the body and has given greater honor to the parts that lacked it, 25so that there should be no division in the body, but that its parts should have equal concern for each other. My right hand is my dominant hand. Some time back, I cut my hand and I was unable to use it. I felt lost and not in control because I use my right hand for practically everything. During this time, I made the necessary adjustments, depending on my left hand, and tasks I thought in the beginning would be difficult, doing them often as my dominant hand healed became easier. We learn to do what we have to do in our time of need. God has given us knowledge on the inside of us that we have never tapped into. What is holding you back, from being and doing all that God has assigned to your hands?

❦ PRAYER ❦
✺✺✺✺✺✺

Lord I am available to you. Father my soul belongs to you. Heavenly Father thank you, for your love and patience with me. Thank you Lord for your continual grace and mercy. Thank you Lord for all that you are doing in the lives of your children. Lord, give us the strength to walk in our calling you've ordained. Lord, you have given us freely everything we need to live a life that is pleasing to you. Lord we realize that trials will come, but we have a solid rock in you to lean upon. Father we honor you, praise you and bless your Holy name. Lord help us to reach down on the inside of our souls and tap into our God given potential. Help us to stir up our gifts. Lord you have already given to your children all that we need to live the good and prosperous life. Lord, we're after your righteousness. Father help us to look at ourselves and see the masterpiece you have created for your continual glory. Oh God, help us to speak positive words over ourselves and others. These precious blessings we ask in your Holy name, Amen.

LISTENING WITH A PURPOSE

Sally and Tasha sit together in church every Sunday; they both hear the same message. Sally is maturing in her faith and learning how to walk in the Spirit, and it is obvious to others that her life is fruitful and productive. Tasha is not growing in the things of God; her life is not productive, and she is not maturing in her faith-walk. How can this paradox be explained? Could it be that we come to God with a certain mind set? Do we have selective listening? Do we decide in advance what we want from scripture and we have a mindset to ignore what we do not want? We must pray and communicate with God before we get to church on Sunday. Our hearts and minds must be receptive to receive from God. Being a Christian is a life style not just a Sunday morning experience.

Matthew 13:1-9 (ESV) *¹That same day Jesus went out of the house and sat beside the sea. ²And great crowds gathered about him, so that he got into a boat and sat down. And the whole crowd stood on the beach. ³And he told them many things in parables, saying: A sower went out to sow. ⁴And as he sowed, some seeds fell along the path, and the birds came and devoured them. ⁵Other seeds fell on rocky ground, where they did not have much soil, and immediately they sprang up, since they had no depth of soil, ⁶but when the sun rose they were scorched. And since they had no root, they withered away. ⁷Other seeds fell among thorns, and the thorns grew up and choked them. ⁸Other seeds fell on good soil and produced grain, some a hundredfold, some sixty, some thirty. ⁹He who has ears, l et him hear.*

I believe that sometimes people can hear the Word and not understand it. When that happens, the enemy will come and quickly steal what they have heard. A type of hearer is the hearer that is closed-minded. This can apply to people who attend church often, but they just choose what they want to take away from the word. Satan will do all he can to divert our attention away from God and His Word. Some people sit Sunday after Sunday and listen passively to God's Word and have no intention of applying what they have heard to their lives. Life is a never-ending series of choices. ***Jeremiah 29:11(KJV)*** *For I know the thoughts that I think toward you, says the Lord, thoughts of peace and not of evil, to give you a future and a hope.* God also wants us to be fulfilled, blessed and successful in the plan that He has established for our lives, so that we can be a reflection of His love and blessing in the Earth. Our Lord and Savior makes clear His intentions for you and me.

God wants to fellowship and communicate with us. That's a two-way communication. God and man; He loves us so much that He sent Jesus to take our place and to die for us. He did this so that we could once again have fellowship with Him. Hold Fast your confession. According to **Hebrews 10: 19-20** *19Therefore, brethren, having boldness to enter the Holiest by the blood of Jesus, 20by a new and living way which He consecrated for us, through the veil, that is, His flesh.* The Lord manifests Himself to us and through us as we humbly seek Him, but I believe some people have a poor image of God, and put God in a box, and define God as they think He should be. We serve a BIG GOD. He is limitless; without walls and this is applicable in your life if you seek Him and get to know Him - not just to know some facts about Him. **Proverbs (KJV) 3:5-6** *⁵Trust in the Lord with all your heart, and lean not on your own understanding; ⁶In all your ways acknowledge Him, And He shall direct your paths.* **Proverbs (NKJV) 11:14** *where no counsel is, the people fall: but in the multitude of counselors there is safety.*

Matthew 18:16(KJV) *And I say also unto thee, That thou art Peter, and upon this rock I will build my church; and the gates of hell shall not prevail against it.*

PRAYER

Heavenly Father I am so grateful for this new day. Thank you Lord for life, health and strength. Thank you for being so good to me and my family. Thank you Lord for family and friends. Father, thank you for your daily grace and mercy that you have bestowed upon me. Lord help me to live for today and not worry about tomorrow, Lord you said in your word, tomorrow has enough trouble of its own. Lord sometimes I get overwhelmed and discouraged with the cares of this world, but I know you are my anchor and strength. Father thank you for teaching me how to encourage myself. Create in me a pure and clean heart. Lord forgive me for times, I have disappointed you, and said things that are contrary to your word. Lord keep me in your divine will. Lord continue to give me the power to do your will. Lord help me not to focus on myself, but focus on others that may need my help. Father look upon the sick in mind and body, heal the broken hearted, take away all fears and doubts. Lord help us to say what your word says about us. Father we are the righteousness of God, and in you we have life. Lord we love you and we honor you. Lord be with the bereaved families, Lord let them know that you are to wise to make a mistake. These peaceful blessings we ask in your Holy name, Amen.

FACE TO FACE WITH THE ENEMY

What are strong holds? When I think of strong holds, I think of wilderness mentality. A stronghold is a negative thinking pattern based on lies and deception. Deception is one of the primary weapons of the devil, because it is the building blocks for a stronghold. What strongholds can do is cause us to think in ways which block us from God's best. Ex: Everyone is against me, no one likes me.

In the book of 1Samuel, David is on the run from King Saul who is trying to kill him. According to

I Samuel (KJV) 23:14 And David abode in the wilderness in strong holds, and remained in a mountain in the wilderness of Ziph. And Saul sought him every day, but God delivered him not into his hand.

Ephesians (KJV) 6:12 For we wrestle not against flesh and blood, but against principalities, against powers, against the rulers of the darkness of this world, against spiritual wickedness in high places.

Have you ever found yourself saying, "Well, I tend to respond that way because my mother did or my father did, or because that is my normal reaction?" Or, "I'm not surprised that happened, my horoscope said this or that." "Heart disease runs in our family; most of my family members have died because of heart disease." We tend to often define truth by reality. God defines truth by His word. But we tend to define truth by what we have experienced. The reality around us. We let that become truth.

According to *2 Corinthians 10:3-5 (KJV) 3For though we walk in the flesh, we do not war after the flesh:(For the weapons of our warfare are not carnal, but mighty through God to the pulling down of strong holds;) Casting down imaginations, and every high thing that exalteth itself against the knowledge of God, and bringing into captivity every thought to the obedience of Christ;*

But God's word is the truth regarding sanctification and holiness, and the ability to be a new creation.

Our realty doesn't change that truth. The righteous trusts not in this; not his own name, but the name of his God, not his own character, but the character of the Most High is his strong tower. Failure plays right out of unbelief. It shows itself in thoughts like, "I will always be a failure," "I'm just a sinner," or "I tried walking in the Spirit, but it didn't work." Have you ever said any of those things about yourself? Have you ever thought them? STOP! One of the most devastating strongholds to have, is an incorrect image in your mind of who God is, and how He sees us. People who see God as a taskmaster, live their lives with an unhealthy fear of God. There's a good kind of fear of God, which is more like a holy respect for Him, but there's another kind of fear that is very unhealthy that the enemy wants us to have, and it's the kind of fear where we see God as a taskmaster, cruel, cold, distant, uncaring and would snap the whip at us the moment we step out of line.

Philippians 4:13 (KJV) *I can do all things through Him who strengthens me.* That is hardly the verse of a failure. Paul says to take every thought captive to the obedience of Christ. We need to capture the thought, "I am a failure!" We need to repent of it. We need to tear down that stronghold with scripture. Capture the thought, "I am just a sinner." We need to repent of it. Tear it down with a verse like ***I John 1:9,*** *Though I was a sinner, now I am a beloved child of God and, though I occasionally still sin, the blood of Christ cleanses me of all unrighteousness.* We need to capture those thoughts of defeat, those thoughts of oppression, those thoughts of failure, and replace them with scriptures like **Romans 8:29** *Whom He foreknew, He also predestined to become conformed to the image of His Son, that He might be the first-born among many brethren."*

✠PRAYER✠
❋❋❋❋❋

Thank you Lord for the awesome privilege to call you Father. Oh Father, how wonderful it is to call on your Holy and righteous name. Lord thank you for your forgiveness of our sins; Father the enemy has lied to us long enough. We know in you we have hope and a bright future. Lord starting today remove the blinders from our eyes, Lord help us to see ourselves through your eyes. Lord your word says, if we call on you, you will answer us. Father we love you and adore you. Lord we realize that you are a loving and compassionate father to your children. Lord help us to see you as the loving and caring Father that you are. Lord we want to be obedient to our Father, teach us Lord how to pray and what to pray for. In Jesus precious name, Amen.

CHAPTER 6

HEAVEN OR HELL? THE CHOICE IS YOURS!

Why do we sin? Oh yes, we all have sinned!! According to **Romans 3:23 (NKJV)** *for all have sinned and fall short of the glory of God.* Sin gratifies our flesh; it makes us feel good temporarily. I can recall when I was a kid, I enjoyed eating candy. My mom would say to my siblings and Me, "do not touch that candy dish". We could hardly wait until her back was turned as we did the opposite. That forbidden candy tasted so good; however, afterwards sometime it would give us a tummy ache. One always pays a price for sinning. Just as in the natural, we pay a price for our sin. There is a spiritual price that we must pay for not obeying God's commandments. We are free moral agents. God could have made us as robots, but He didn't. We have a choice in the matter.

Romans 3:18 (NIV) *There is no fear of God before their eyes"*. They have no respect for God, our Creator. But the "whole duty of man" is to fear God and keep His commandments. Ecclesiastes 12:13 Before we can keep God's commandments we must know what they are. **Hosea 4:6 (NKJV)** *My people are destroyed for lack of knowledge. Because you have rejected knowledge, I also will reject you from being priest for Me; because you have forgotten the law of your God, I also will forget your children.*

We must develop an awesome respect for God and His word. **1 John 1:8 (ESV)** *If we say we have no sin, we deceive ourselves,* *and the truth is not in us.* When we get to know God and His character, and how much He loves us, we will want to please Him. Therefore, we will spend time in His word getting to know Him. We are deceived by sin. God wants us to exhort one another daily, while it is called today, lest any of you be hardened through the deceitfulness of sin. **Ephesians 5:6** *Let no man deceive you with vain words: for because of these things cometh the wrath of God upon the children of disobedience.*

I believe we sin because there is temporary pleasure in sin. Hebrews 11:25 (KJV) Moses chose "rather to suffer affliction with the people of God, than to enjoy the pleasures of sin for a season. Think about this for a moment. Have you ever decided to cut back on your eating, maybe abstain from sweets? That is the very time you cannot control your craving. you decide to eat just one piece of chocolate and before you know you have eaten the entire bag or close to it.

Because of the pleasures of sin, we are easily enticed. **James 1:14-15 (KJV)** *But every man is tempted, when he is drawn away of his own lust, and enticed. Then when lust hath conceived, it bringeth forth sin: and sin, when it is finished, bringeth forth death.*
   Proverbs (KJV) 21:10 *The soul of the wicked desireth evil: his neighbour findeth no favour in his eyes.*

1 Corinthians 15:33 (KJV) *Be not deceived: evil communications corrupt good manners."* People sin because of the influence of the people with whom they associate. Be mindful of your friends, day and night are opposite of each other." , "Do not be deceived evil company corrupts good habits". Again, we must carefully choose our associates. **1 Thessalonians 5:22 (NKJV)** *Abstain from every form of evil.* We are not perfect but we are striving to be more like our father."

 PRAYER

Heavenly Father, thank you for your daily blessings that you have bestowed upon me. Thank you Lord for this day allowing me another opportunity to praise your Holy and righteous name. Father, you are more than good to your children. Lord, we all have sinned and fallen short of your glory but your love for us has never changed nor has your compassion. Lord, you are a Father that will never change. I am so thankful and grateful that you call me your child. Lord, bless everyone praying this prayer and help them to resist every evil temptation that is contrary to your will. Lord, give your children the desire to spend more intimate time with you. These precious things we ask in your name. Amen.

PREREQUISET FOR LOVING

For a long time, I was ashamed of my past. I did not want others to judge me because of my past mistakes. I lived to please others. Today my validation comes from God and Him alone. Some of my past experiences were not good, but the important thing is I have a bright future and the lessons I have learned are priceless. The Lord has changed my life forever in a way I never could have imagined. I feared be rejected and shun by others. I know who I am in God; God has given me a new outlook and a new identity. I am still a work in progress, I still have issues, I have not arrived yet, but with God all things are possible and I am still striving to be the best person, I can be with the help of the Holy Spirit. God loves me too much to leave me as I am. We cannot truly love others until we love ourselves.

I can honestly say today without a doubt, I love myself. Sometimes we use the word love so loosely. **Genesis 1:26 (NKJV)** *Then God said, Let Us make man in Our image, according to Our likeness; let them have dominion over the fish of the sea, over the birds of the air, and over the cattle, over all the earth and over every creeping thing that creeps on the earth.* I remember running from a dog as a child, I fell and cut my foot, every day I am aware of that incident because of the scar on my foot. My foot no longer hurts because it has healed. Our life is the same way, when we experience hurt, and disappointments God will heal those places if we allow Him to.

Luke 13:11-16 (NKJV) And behold, there was a woman who had a spirit of infirmity eighteen years, and was bent over and could in no way raise herself up. But when Jesus saw her, He called her to Him and said to her, "Woman, you are loosed from your infirmity. And He laid His hands on her, and immediately she was made straight, and glorified God. When God put His hand of approval on us, we are new creatures in Him, and all things become new; our old man no longer exist. I had a hard time letting go of the old Patricia, the selfish and self-centered Patricia that God made new. I had to make a choice, I could take God at His word and believe what God said about me, or stay within the old mind set. I chose to accept God's forgiveness, then I forgave myself. At that point and time in my life I was able to move forward. **Proverbs 19:8 (NKJV)** *He who gets wisdom loves his own soul; He who keeps understanding will find good..* you see our thinking pattern gets confused. So often we put ourselves down and we don't feel good about ourselves and then that clouds everything we do. Most of those things we struggle with is not because we can't do them;. It's because we think we're not capable of doing things. Self-image is your judgment of yourself. It is your picture of yourself. It is your opinion of yourself. Learn to say what God says about you. Practice, Practice and Practice the word of God! If you cannot love yourself, you will not be able to love other people and you will not be able to love God. So everything depends on this thing called self-image. Self-image will not be neutral in your life. It is incredibly powerful. It will be your greatest asset or it will be your worst enemy, but it will not be neutral.

Psalm 139:13-15 (NKJV) *For you formed my inward parts; you covered me in my mother's womb.*

I will praise you, for I am fearfully and wonderfully made; Marvelous are your works, And that my soul knows very well. My frame was not hidden from you, When I was made in secret, And skillfully wrought in the lowest parts of the earth. When our love tanks are full, we have the energy and patience to give love to the world around us; but when we are running on empty, that's how we feel: empty. With an empty love tank, we feel overwhelmed, frustrated, angry, and sad, you name it and that's how we treat others, which can ultimately lessen their love tanks too. I want to challenge each of you to hug yourself every day and remind yourself that everything God made was good. I believe it starts with loving God and yourself. ***John 15:9 (NKJV)*** *As the Father loved Me, I also have loved you; abide in My love.*

✣❬PRAYER❭✣
✤✤✤✤✤✤

Thank you Father God for this day. Thank you Lord for your love and divine favor on my life. Lord, thank you for watching over my family and me as we slept through the night. Thank you Heavenly Father for keeping me in my right mind. Oh God how I love and adore you. Lord I realize today that nothing will happen to me today that you and I cannot handle. Father my life is not my own. I live for you, and it is to you I belong. Lord forgive me of my sins and any thoughts or responses that is contrary to you. Create in me a pure and clean heart. Lord thank you for your faithfulness and love for me. Lord give me the strength I need to do your will. Lord help me to love others and myself with the love you shower me with daily. Father touch the brokenhearted; heal the sick bodies, and double mindedness of your children. Lord I stand against mental illness, worry, depression, confusion, slothfulness and stagnation. Lord you have provided all that we need to live a fruitful and productive life. Lord help your people to stand and be bold declaring your word. Lord continue to bless your people with whatever they stand in need of, in Jesus Holy and righteous name, Amen.

WE HAVE NOTHING TO FEAR BUT FEAR IN SELF

In one of my classes at Webster University, my instructor passed out his syllabus and stated, "Starting today, everyone has an A in this class, but it is up to you to keep it." My heart began to pound and my hands started to sweat. My first thought was, "How can I maintain an A with all that is expected of me?" I realized that my feelings of desperation were the result of my fear of failure. **2 Timothy 1:7** *For God hath not given us the spirit of fear; but of power, and of love, and of a sound mind.* Fear is one of the things the enemy uses to discourage the children of God; but in God, we have an anchor. Hold on to God and do not let Him go. I do not have to work for God's approval. He died for my sins that set me free. I still have those days when I look at the things that I have not done well and begin to drown myself in guilt. On the other hand, I have those days that I look at what I have done well and begin to think I have myself together. When I hit these extremes, God reminds me, He is my pilot and He is doing the driving. I have to remind myself that my relationship with God is not based on my performance. I am what I am (a new creation) not because of anything I have done, but because of what God has done for me. He removed the threat of failure. **John 14:1** *Let not your hearts be troubled. Believe in God believe also in me.*

According to **Psalm 23:1-6 (NKJV)** *The Lord is my shepherd; I shall not want. He makes me to lie down in green pastures; He leads me beside the still waters. He restores my soul; He leads me in the paths of righteousness for His name sake. Yea, though I walk through the valley of the shadow of death, I will fear no evil; for you are with me; your rod and your staff, they comfort me. You prepare a table before me in the presence of my enemies; you anoint my head with oil; my cup runs over. Surely goodness and mercy shall follow me all the days of my life; And I will dwell in the house of the Lord Forever.*

Because of the promise of God, we can now, relax and enjoy our relationship with our heavenly father. I am so thankful that on my worst days I am not beyond the reach of God's grace.

On our best days, we are never so good that, we are beyond the need of God's grace and direction.

Proverbs 3:5 (NKJV) *Trust in the Lord with all your heart and lean not on your own understanding.* Our own goodness does not lead us to the goodness of God. We are born into sin; we all are sinners, in need of a savior. We must learn to rely on God. Relying on our father's strength and His power keeps us feeding on His goodness and keeping our source aligned with it daily. God is GOOD. He is good all the time, it is vital to understand that He doesn't love us in word only. He loves us with action. God's love and His goodness are inseparable. When you know God loves you, and when you know He is good, you can always rest in the arms of Jesus. Pleasing God is, or should be, the goal of all believers. According to **Romans 8:8 (NKJV)** *So then, those who are in the flesh cannot please God.*

The first step in pleasing God is to accept the sacrifice for sin that He provided in the death of Jesus Christ on the cross. Only then are we "in the Spirit" and not in the flesh. Hebrews 11:6(NIV) tells us "And without faith it is impossible to please God, because anyone who comes to him must believe that he exists and that he rewards those who earnestly seek him." Furthermore, we must live by faith as God cannot be pleased with those who "shrink back" from Him, because they have no confidence in Him; they doubt the truth of His declarations and promises; or do not believe that His ways are right and holy and perfect. Faith and confidence in God is not unreasonable; it is just what we require of our children and spouses; and it is an indispensable condition of our being pleased with them. **John 14:15 (NIV)** *If you love me, you will keep my commands."* Therefore, pleasing God is a matter of living according to His manual (The Holy Bible) commandments, and doing so in love. We desire to please those we love. The Bible is full with exhortations to righteous living and loving God by obeying His commandments

⚡PRAYER⚡
✽✽✽✽✽✽

Thank you, Lord, for your unconditional love. Lord, thank you for loving me, when I did not love myself. Thank you for not giving up on me. Lord, all that I am, and all that I hope to be is because of you. Father, in all I do, I honor you. God is love, He wants what is best for his children, and He is our creator. God desires His children to live a good life, a life without guilt and shame. God wants His children to trust Him and believe He is who He said He is. Oh Holy and gracious Father, thank you for this day. Thank you, Lord, for all that you are doing in the life of your children. Lord, continue to bless us, and help us to see ourselves as you see us. These blessing we ask in your precious name, Amen.

MY FIRST LOVE

In the early 80's there was a song titled, "My First Love" by: Rene and Angela. Some of the lyrics were As long as I live you will always be my first love. Who was your first love? Hum! God desires to be our first real love. God is in pursuit of every believer. He created us for His purpose, and we get to participate with Him in doing something significant for His Kingdom. Seeking God's will should be a joyful process not a burdensome task. We can enjoy the journey and shake off guilt, pain, and past failures. When we seek an intimate relationship with God, we can settle into a peace that surpasses all human understanding. Without God's guidance, we sometimes view our lives as a puzzle, however with God and the help of the Holy Spirit we can locate the missing pieces and explore the big picture. We sometimes used the word love with no thought of what it really means. As human beings we tend to mimic the behavior of others and not God. Remember, love is what links us together and draws others to Christ.

John 16:13 (NKJV) *However, when He, the Spirit of truth, has come, He will guide you into all truth; for He will not speak on His own authority, but whatever He hears He will speak; and He will tell you things to come.* God does not love us because we are lovable or because we deserve His love. If anything, the opposite is true.

According to *Jeremiah 17:9 (NKJV)* *The heart is deceitful above all things, and desperately wicked: who can know it?* God's nature is love. Love is embodied in His very being and woven into all His other attributes; and we're created in that. We deserve to give God all glory and praise.

1John 4:10(NKJV) *In this is love, not that we loved God, but that He loved us and sent His Son to be the propitiation for our sins.*

Nothing sinful or evil can exist in our heavenly father He is absolutely good. He cannot, and will not overlook, condone, or excuse sin as if it never happened. God will forgive our sins, when we come to Him and sincerely repent of our wrong doing. He loves us, but His love does not make Him turn a blind side to our sin. I am the righteousness of God and Christ; therefore, I can produce right behavior, with God, I can do all things. When we totally trust in God, we do not have to carry the weight of our sins.

Romans 5:8 (NKJV) *But God demonstrates His own love toward us, in that while we were still sinners, Christ died for us.*

God's love is personal. He knows each of us individually and loves us personally. His is God's love is personal. He knows each of us by name, just as He knows each strain of hair on our heads. His love is everlasting and has no end.

Ephesians 2:4–5(NKJV) *But God, who is rich in mercy, because of His great love with which He loved us, 5 even when we were dead in trespasses, made us alive together with Christ (by grace you have been saved).* God's love does not come with a condition. If God's love were conditional, then we would have to do something to earn it. What an awesome father we serve.

Deuteronomy 6:5(NKJV) *You shall love the Lord your God with all your heart, with all your soul, and with all your strength.* We can do nothing without the help of our Father and the Holy Spirit. As we grow in the things of Christ and witness His compassion, His grace, His love for us, His hatred for sin, His holiness and righteousness, we love Him more and more. We cannot love someone we don't know, so knowing Him should be our first priority. Thank you Lord.

PRAYER
✱✱✱✱✱

Most Holy and everlasting father thank you for this day. Lord allow your un-conditional love to fill me up, and for its presence to encourage others to do the same .Father allow kindness and compassion to come alive in the souls where it has grown dark. Lord help me to use the power that you have given me to break the chains and walls that keep me from being the person I was made to be. Father help me to see myself through your eyes. Oh God help us to remember the greatest gift we can give to others is to love them, because you first loved us. Help me to allow happiness and joy to be mine today and every day. Lord I love you and desire to please you. Lord help us in every area of our lives. Lord we realize that without love we are like a ship without a sail, tossing to and fro. Lord help us to remember we are accountable for how we treat others, not how others may treat us. Lord help us to be authentic and not superficial in all that we do. In Jesus mighty name, Amen.

Chapter 7

TEAR DOWN TO REBUILD

During my time in prayer and meditation, I heard the Lord say to me, tear down to rebuild. When God speaks, He is very clear and concise. Thanks be to God, I have an ear to hear what the Spirit of the Lord has to say to me. When I was a child, a family friend would visit us often, we called him UL, and his job title was a demolitionist. As a curious teen, I asked him what that meant. His response was "I tear down mostly old buildings that are no longer needed, or functional. I looked up the definition of demolition it is as follows. The tearing-down of buildings and other structures. Demolition contrasts with deconstruction, which involves taking a building apart while carefully preserving valuable elements for re-use. God desires to tear down all that is within us that is not functioning properly, to restore and rebuild. When we try to function in the old and God is trying to move us into the new, we are headed for destruction. God is so crafty, He can love on us, chastise us and never bruise us. What an awesome father. I enjoy looking in magazines at old dilapidated houses and furniture that have been restored or rebuilt. In some cases by looking at the old, we sometimes visualize the possibilities of something new. Ask the Lord to open your eyes to new possibilities and new direction. Sometimes we are looking and unable to see.

Isaiah 9:10 (KJV) The bricks have fallen, but we will build with dressed stones; the sycamores have been cut down, but we will put cedars in their place. I believe when God want to do a new thing in the lives of His people, He will orchestrate situations and circumstances in our lives the make us uncomfortable. We will step up to the challenge, find fault with others or remain where we are. What will your decision be today?

1 Peter 2:5 (NIV) You yourselves like living stones are being built up as a spiritual house, be a holy priesthood, to offer spiritual sacrifices acceptable to God through Jesus Christ. God desires to tear down anything that may be interfering with our growth and preventing us from doing His will. This could be a lot of different things, family, jobs, friends, hatred that we may have against others, jealously, and are envy etc. God will do for us, what He has given us the ability to do for ourselves. We must learn to let go and let God. We have so much potential that God has given us that we have never tapped into.

According to *Jeremiah 31:3, The Lord has appeared of old to me, saying: "Yes, I have loved you with an everlasting love; Therefore with loving kindness I have drawn you.* God loves us to much to leave us the way that we are. We are a continued work in progress.

Pleasing God should be our first priority. When our way pleases the Lord, God almighty He will make even our enemies to be at peace with us. Lord we welcome you to do a new thing in our lives, we welcome you to transform our mind and hearts.

Psalm 150:1-6 (NKJV) *Praise the Lord! Praise God in His sanctuary; Praise Him in His mighty firmament! Praise Him for His mighty acts; Praise Him according to His excellent greatness! Praise Him with the sound of the trumpet; Praise Him with the lute and harp! Praise Him with the timbrel and dance; Praise Him with stringed instruments and flutes! Praise Him with loud cymbals; Praise Him with clashing cymbals! Let everything that has breath praise the Lord. Praise the Lord.*

PRAYER

Lord thank you for this day. Thank you Lord for all of your many, many blessings that you have bestowed upon me and my family. Lord help us to envision the possibilities that you have in store for your children. Lord, we know that all things work together for the good to them that love the Lord and are called according to His purpose. Lord you are an awesome Father to your children. Lord help us to praise you when we are happy as well as when things are going contrary to our plan. We realize that praise ushers us into your presence. We thank you Father for loving us, leading us as you would have us go. Lord we welcome you to take our blinders off and allow us to see the beauty within us. Lord mold us and shape us into your will, father enlarge our territory. These precious blessings we ask in your Holy and sanctified name, Amen.

ARE YOU A VISIONARY?

Daniel 10:7-11(NKJV) *And I Daniel alone saw the vision: for the men that were with me saw not the vision; but a great quaking fell upon them, so that they fled to hide themselves. Therefore I was left alone, and saw this great vision, and there remained no strength in me: for my comeliness was turned in me into corruption, and I retained no strength. Yet heard I the voice of his words: and when I heard the voice of his words, then was I in a deep sleep on my face, and my face toward the ground. And, behold, an hand touched me, which set me upon my knees and upon the palms of my hands. And he said unto me, O Daniel, a man greatly beloved, understand the words that I speak unto thee, and stand upright: for unto thee am I now sent. And when he had spoken this word unto me, I stood trembling.*

Daniel the prophet receives a word from the Lord, a vision of conflict that stunned him with its greatness. So Daniel set himself with tears, fasting and prayer to seek the meaning of the vision; for three weeks he wrestled in prayer over this vision and sought to know God's will. Sometimes because of our fears, hurts, disappointments and disobedience when we pray we feel God does not hear our prayers. ***Habakkuk 2:3(KJV)*** *For the vision is yet for an appointed time, but at the end it shall speak, and not lie: though it tarry, wait for it; because it will surely come, it will not tarry.* Sometimes others cannot see the vision God has given to you, and therefore others cannot share your vision. When God gives you a vision, you may have to walk that road out alone.

Daniel 10:12 (KJV) *Then said he unto me, Fear not, Daniel: for from the first day that thou didst set thine heart to understand, and to chasten thyself before thy God, thy words were heard, and I am come for thy* *words.* When we get in the presence of God we must humble ourselves as a little child and give God the honor due him. Like myself and many of you; have been praying and asking the Lord for certain things, it may appear as if our prayers are not being answered. But we remain hopeful. When we get dishearten, we can think back on Daniel. If God answered Daniel he will answer us. The Lord has no respecter of person. Do you have a vision or a promise from God? Hold on to your miracle and promise. It is closer than you think. Stay in the race. In the mean while continue to do what God has assign your hands to do while you wait for the vision to come to past.

Daniel was frightened by his vision, but the messenger's hand calmed his fears; Daniel lost his speech, but the messenger's words strengthened him. God will bring us healing when we hurt, peace when we are troubled, and strength when we are weak. God knows we face the same challenges as Daniel did. Daniel cried, he fasted and he sought God. There is a price for God's anointing. Are you willing? God's timing is not like ours. Remember your words have power and God hears our prayers the first time we pray. There are seasons we must go through before we can receive some things God has promised us; but we are never alone. I want to encourage you to never give up and know God is true and faithful to his word.

Psalm 23:2 (KJV) *He maketh me to lie down in green pastures: he leadeth me beside the still waters.* You see sheep are dumb stubborn creatures. They don't have enough sense to know when to lie down to rest so there are times that He makes me lie down but the good thing is that He makes me lie down where the green pastures are. That is where I can be fed on the Word of God. Sheep have been known to stay in one place and eat until they eat down to the dirt. A good shepherd moves them to green pastures. Sheep is about the dumbest of all of God's creatures and we are like sheep, at times, Isaiah 53:6 All we like sheep have gone astray; we have turned everyone to his own way; and the LORD hath laid on him the iniquity of us all." To various degrees we all go through the valleys of what seem to be immediate death at times. God never said He would keep us out of these valleys of death or stop us from going through them, but He said that He will go "through the valley" with us." What an awesome assurance. If God has given you a vision, hold on, believe it and know He will come through for you. He is God and He cannot lie. The enemy will come, but we have God's word and His promise.

PRAYER

Great is the Lord, and greatly to be praised. Lord thank you for providing my every need. Father God guard my heart and mind from all unrighteousness. Lord you are so worthy to be praise. Thank you for family and friends. Lord, I love and adore you. Lord I pray your continual blessing on the life of your children. Lord enlarge our territories. Father so many times we are guilty of putting you in a box, because our vision is too small. Lord there is none that can be compare to you. Lord, look upon the eyes, minds and hearts of your people, give us comfort, and insight like you did for Daniel. Lord, strengthen us, and give us your divine peace that only you can provide. These precious blessing I ask in your name, Amen.

COME LORD JESUS COME

God is awesome and He is worthy of our praise. Our praise team sang a song recently and some of the words are, "all I need to do is worship, all I need to lift my hands and surrender and bow down." God wants our praise. The Pastor's message was entitled The House Call. That word was very encouraging to me, and I am sure to others as well. The Lord put in my spirit "Come Lord Jesus Come." I want the Lord to come, come into my heart, come into my mind, and come into every part of my being. "Come Lord Jesus Come." ***Psalm 8:1(Holman Christian Bible)*** *Lord our Lord, how magnificent is your name throughout the earth! You have covered the heavens with your majesty.* Praise is expressing to God our appreciation and understanding of Him. It is saying "thank you" for each aspect of His divine nature. Our inward attitude becomes outward expression. When we praise God, we help ourselves by expanding our awareness of who He is.

Psalm 9:1-2 (Holman Christian Bible) *I will thank the Lord my God with all my heart; I will declare all his wonderful works. I will rejoice and boast about you; I will sing about your name, Most High.* One of the natural marks of praising God is witnessing. When we know God is wonderful, we naturally want to tell others and have them praise God with us. God desires to have intimacy with His children. We all face trials and obstacles, but God has promised never to leave us alone. STOP looking at the size of the mountain and focus on the mountain maker. Don't focus on the crisis, rather focus on the Christ that will remove the crisis! We are to praise God in season and out of season. O LORD our Lord, how excellent is thy name in all the earth!

There is something about calling on the name of Jesus that brings a calmness to our inner spirit. I challenge you to stop where you are if you can, and just begin to call on the name of Jesus. I promise you He will come! ***Psalm 10:1 (NKJV)*** *Why standest thou afar off, O Lord? Why hidest thou thyself in times of trouble?* Sometimes when we face challenges, we feel God is far away, but on the contrary He is right there beside you, holding you up and carrying you. The more we stay in His word, seek Him and talk to Him the more evident His presence is revealed to us. Psalm 143:7 (Holman Christian Bible) "Answer me quickly, Lord; my spirit fails. Don't hide your face from me, or I will be like those going down to the Pit."

Psalm 91:1-4 (KJV) *He that dwelleth in the secret place of the most High shall abide under the shadow of the Almighty. I will say of the Lord, He is my refuge and my fortress: my God; in him will I trust. Surely he shall deliver thee from the snare of the fowler, and from the noisome pestilence. He shall cover thee with his feathers, and under his wings shalt thou trust: his truth shall be thy shield and buckler.* God promises great blessings to His people. He will free us from fear, deliver us from trouble, protect us from harm, show us kindness, supply our needs, listen when we talk to Him and redeem us from the hand of the enemy. We can appropriate His blessing when we seek Him, cry out to Him and trust Him and have humble hearts.

PRAYER

Lord thank you for your awesomeness. Father God thank you for this new day. Lord thank you for your goodness and daily mercies that you bestow upon me. I need you to come Lord Jesus come; come to my rescue.

Lord you are an amazing father, comforter, healer, encourager, protector and heart fixer. Lord thank you for opening doors I could not see, thank you Lord for friends and family. Lord thank you for every trial which never feels good; but I realize you work things out for my good. Lord help us to lean and depend on you and you alone. Lord give me the strength to persevere on days that are challenging to me. Lord my life would be nothing without you. Thank you Lord for loving me, thank you Lord for being forever good to me. Thank you Lord for where you brought me from and for where you are taking me. These peaceful blessings I ask in your Holy name, Amen.

MAXIMIZE GOD'S PRECIOUS GIFT OF TIME

Time is a precious gift that God has given to each of us. Time is something we can never get back once it has past. A former pastor said to me once, "I don't allow others to waste my time." I have heard it said that there is not enough time in a day to accomplish everything on my agenda. I would like to suggest that you change your agenda just for today. Ask God for His wisdom in creating a plan that works for you.

Ephesians (ESV) 5:15 – 17 *Look carefully then how you' walk, not as unwise but as wise, making the best use of the time, because the days are evil. Therefore do not be foolish, but understand what the will of the Lord is.*

We say with such assurance, we will do this or that

tomorrow, how do we know what tomorrow will bring? Lord teach us to maximize this moment, because tomorrow I may never see. Every moment is a gift, I challenge you treat it as the gift that it is.

James 4:13-17(ESV) Come now, you who say, Today or tomorrow we will go into such and such a town and spend year there and trade and make a profit yet you do not know what tomorrow will bring. What is your life? For you are a mist that appears for a little time and then vanishes. Instead you ought to say, "If the Lord wills, we will live and do this or that." As it is, you boast in your arrogance. All such boasting is evil. So whoever knows the right thing to do and fails to do it, for him it is sin.

God is the only one that knows what tomorrow will bring. The Bible says that our days are numbered.

According to **Psalm 39:4-5 (KJV)** *Lord, make me to know my end, And what is the measure of my days, That I may know how frail I am. Indeed, you have made my days as handbreadths, And my age is as nothing before you; Certainly every man at his best state is but vapor.*

Ephesians 4:15 (NIV) *Instead, speaking the truth in love, we will in all things grow up into him who is the Head, that is, Christ.*

We must know our purpose. Everything that we do or attempt to do should have a God given purpose. **Matthew 6:33 (KJV)**, *But seek ye first the kingdom of God, and his righteousness; and all these things shall be added unto you.*

It is wise to plan, but allow God to be in the center of your plan. He is the author and the finisher or all planning. I have heard it said, you need to hope for the best, but plan for the worst.

Luke 14:18-29 (NIV) *Suppose one of you wants to build a tower. Won't you first sit down and estimate the cost to see if you have enough money to complete it? For if you lay the foundation and are not able to finish it, everyone who sees it will ridicule you, saying, this person began to build and wasn't able to finish.*

Have you counted the cost of poor planning? Someone said, "If you fail to plan, you plan to fail. "Would you plan a trip without knowing which road to travel or how long it will take you to get there? When I look at my grandchildren from day to day I often wonder where has the time gone. I remember putting diapers on them, and now they are driving, graduating from school and preparing for college. Time waits on no one. Time can be your friend or an enemy. Consult God for His divine intervention and His strategic wisdom. ***Job 9:25 (NIV)*** *Now my days are swifter than a post they flee away, they see no good. They are passed away as the swift ships: as the eagle that hasteth to the prey.* We do not have time for pettiness, things that are no value to the kingdom of God. Time is short, sweet and precious. We have so much to do for the Kingdom of God. Patience is power. Patience is not a lack of action; relatively it is "timing."

PRAYER
✸✸✸✸✸

Father thank you for the gift of time. Thank you Lord for this precious day. Lord help me to maximize every minute of each day that you allow me to see. Lord help me to consult you and your direction for my time. Father I desire you to be in the center of all my plans. Lord you said in your word that you would order my steps and keep me in perfect peace if I keep my mind stayed on you. Father when I am tempted to worry, get overly excited, or get into the way, keep me focused and grounded through your word. Lord sometimes I am impatient and want things to happen right away, but I know your timing may not be my timing. Help me to lean and depend on you and your word. Psalm 37:4 tells me to delight myself in you and you will give me the desires of my heart. Lord teach me to wait on the hope and promises we have in you. Lord help me to plan, and prioritize time, but most of all help me to seek you and your direction and will for my life. In Jesus glorious name, Amen.

GOD REQUIRE FAITHFULNESS

God desires you to succeed in everything you do! According to **Jeremiah 29:11 (NKJV)** *For I know the thoughts that I think toward you, says the Lord, thoughts of peace and not of evil, to give you a future and a hope."*

There have been times in my life, I have prayed and God answered me quickly, then there have been other times I prayed and it felt like God turned a deaf ear to my prayer. God always answers our prayers, in one of three ways, Yes, No and Wait, not yet. We must learn to be content with whatever His answer is to our prayer request. In my life, I struggle when I am waiting on God, although I know that God's timing is perfect. I know God has a perfect plan for my life, and I know without a doubt that God loves me. I am a continual work in progress. Sometimes we tend to want to fix things and make things happen. From experience, when I went ahead of God, I would end up disappointed, disillusioned and often hurt. **Psalm 40:1** *I waited patiently for the LORD; and he inclined unto me, and heard my cry.*

In our lives, our faith will be tested, which allows us to grow in our relationship with our Heavenly Father. God is always faithful, He knows everything in the past, present, and future. He knows about our needs as well as our wants and desires. God can do all things, accomplish anything because He is all-powerful. We will prosper in every area of our lives when we are faithful.

When I think of faithfulness, my mind reflects back to the faithfulness of my earthly father. My Dad provided for his children, even when he was faced with difficult circumstances. My Dad's word was his bond. He believed in keeping his word. He was a man of integrity although he never confessed being a Christian. I looked up the word faithfulness and according to

Wikipedia - Faithfulness is the concept of unfailingly remaining loyal to someone or something and putting that loyalty into consistent practice, regardless of extenuating circumstances. God wants us to be transparent and authentic. *Deuteronomy 7:9 (NKJV) Therefore know that the Lord your God, He is God, the faithful God who keeps covenant and mercy for a thousand generations with those who love Him and keep His commandments.*

Malachi 3:6 (NKJV) *For I am the Lord, I do not change; Therefore you are not consumed, O sons of Jacob.* God never changes; His character is the same yesterday, today, and forever. Trust in God's perfect plan for you, Trust in God's perfect purpose for you, and Trust in God's perfect timing. God's character is also essential if we are to understand His faithfulness to us. **Matthew 6:33** *But seek ye first the kingdom of God, and his righteousness; and all these things shall be added unto you.* God will meet all our needs if they are in His divine plan.

According to **2 Corinthians 1:22**, *who also has sealed us and given us the Spirit in our hearts as a guarantee.* God's word is the final authority. **Isaiah 55:10-11 (NKJV)** *10For as the rain comes down, and the snow from heaven, And do not return there, But water the earth, And make it bring forth and bud, That it may give seed to the sower. And bread to the eater 11So shall My word be that goes forth from My mouth; It shall not return to Me void, But it shall accomplish what I please, And it shall prosper in the thing for which I sent it.*

PRAYER

Father thank you for this great day. Thank you Lord for your faithfulness to your children. Lord thank you for being an awesome father to your undeserving children. Lord I need you every moment of every day, Lord I cannot do anything without you. Father forgive me for my sins, create in me a pure and clean heart. Renew a right spirit within me. Lord thank you for keeping me in my right mind. Lord thank you for making me aware of

your presence. Thank you Lord for the gift of your Holy Spirit. Lord help me to be faithful to you and faithful to the commitment I have made to others. Oh God help us to be faithful in every area of our lives. These wonderful blessings I ask in your name, Amen.

Chapter 8

DIFFICULT TIMES PRODUCES GODLY CHARACTER

Hardship often prepares ordinary people for an extraordinary destiny. Life at any moment can end. I made a conscious decision to live and not just exist. **Psalm 23:1(KJV)** *The Lord is my Shepherd I shall not want.* God desires that His children live a life of abundance. In my early adult years, I worked for a family that lived life to the fullest. In my opinion they were living the American dream. They lived in a beautiful home, traveled, and took vacations. Most of all they enjoyed their relationship with God Almighty. I never heard them complain about their finances, or not having enough of anything. I knew they were not rich, but they were comfortable and they also gave to others that were less fortunate. **Ephesians 3:20 (KJV)** *Now unto him that is able to do exceeding* *abundantly above all that we ask or think, according to the power that worketh in us.*

My life is better now than it ever has been, spiritually and in the natural. God does not want His children living a life of lack.
Deuteronomy 28:12 *The Lord shall open unto thee his good treasure, the heaven to give the rain unto thy land in his season, and to bless all the work of thine hand: and thou shalt lend unto many nations, and thou shalt not borrow.*
When we have a relationship with the Heavenly Father; and know who we are in Him and because of Him, we can have whatever we desire. We limit God and ourselves by the way we think and the words we speak. The word of God says, we have not because we ask not. What will you speak today? **2 Corinthians 8:1 (KJV)** *Moreover, brethren, we do you to wit of the grace of God bestowed on the churches of Macedonia; how that in a great trial of affliction the abundance of their joy and their deep poverty abounded unto the riches of their liberality.* Success is not found in money, or in our prize possessions. Real happiness is found in knowing Jesus; and in abundance of love, joy, faith, goodness, respect for others and hope! For many people, life is nothing more than the time spent between being born and their demise. Deuteronomy 28:8a The Lord will send a blessing on your barns and on everything you put your hands to. God's blessings are waiting to overtake you, just ask!

Have you ever wondered, why the more we have, the more we want? I believe that is because, we put our hope in things and not God. **Ecclesiastes 5:10 (KJV)** *He that loveth silver shall not be satisfied with silver; nor he that loveth abundance with increase: this is also vanity.*
One doesn't find life in position. Too often people think that if they receive a certain promotion, or obtain a certain status, or live in a particular neighborhood then they would be happy. Interestingly, those people who have reached that position still have not found the secret of happiness.

Ecclesiastes 1:8 (KJV) *All things are full of labour; man cannot utter it: the eye is not satisfied with seeing, nor the ear filled with hearing.* Some people do not enjoy the pleasures of life. My aunt said to me before she found Christ, "If I did not wake up, it would be ok." My heart ache for her, knowing that she lived such an empty and unfulfilled life. She had so much to give, and so many people whose life could have been better just to have known her. However before her passing, she got to know Jesus and his love for her. My aunt's life was forever changed.

I've heard people say that life is passing them by. I suggest they get to know God. We serve a God who is often referred to the one who meets all our needs, that is very true, but He is a God of more than enough. I have also heard others say, "Our God supplies all our need but not our greed". There are many things said about our God, one thing I know are that we do not serve a frugal God; He gives us more than enough. He is a God of abundance. ***John 14:13-14*** *And whatsoever ye shall ask in my name, that will I do, that the Father may be glorified in the Son. If ye shall ask any thing in my name, I will do it.*

While most of us desire to live a good life and be happy. A good life is defined differently for every individual. I challenge you to allow God to be the beginning. God is happiness. He will give you purpose, joy, hope, and love…….

PRAYER
✸✸✸✸✸

Father thank you for all that you are to me. Thank you for being my, God, my friend and my everything. Thank you Lord for this day, the opportunity to love others and share of your goodness. Lord, I honor you and want my life to bring you glory. Lord we thank you for the gift of life, health and strength. Father we thank you for each breath that sustains life. Lord we thank you for what our eye can see and what our ear can hear. Thank you Lord for surrounding me with your protection and your divine favor. Father continue to bless all your children, help them to live life in the present. Help them dear Lord to live a life of abundance. In Jesus precious name, Amen

ARE YOUR FRUIT BRUISED OR ROTTEN?

I recently had a conversation with a friend; I asked her how is it that people can attend church every week, hear the word of God and not change? Her response was, "they have a reprobate mind." I am in no way judging others; however the bible tells us that a tree is known by the fruit it bears.

Matthew 7:16-20 (KJV) [16]*Ye shall know them by their fruits. Do men gather grapes of thorns, or figs of thistles?* [17]*Even so every good tree bringeth forth good fruit; but a corrupt tree bringeth forth evil fruit.* [18]*A good tree cannot bring forth evil fruit, neither can a corrupt tree bring forth good fruit.* [19]*Every tree that bringeth not forth good fruit is hewn down, and cast into the fire.* [20]*Wherefore by their fruits ye shall know them.* Are the fruit you bearing, bruise, ripe or spoil?

Some Christians find that they have grown very little

spiritually after many years. They may have been a Christian for 20 years but discover that a one-year old Christian is overtaking them in terms of spiritual maturity. I believe this is because some of the veterans Christian have gotten cold spiritually in the things of God. Take for instance you have work on the same job for 10 years, someone new comes to the company, that you are to take under your wings and teach them how things are done from your perspective. Most of the time, we believe that our way of doing things are the best way to do it, however, learning new things is inevitable but growth is choice . The novice Christian is eager to learn all he can about God and his ways, he is open and willing to be taught. He is also willing to invest time in bible study, prayer service, and he spends time studying God's word.

According to ***2 Peter 3:18(KJV)*** *But grow in the grace and knowledge of our Lord and Savior Jesus Christ. To him be glory both now and forever. Amen.*

In the book Folk Psalm of Faith, author Ray Stedman tells a story of a woman who had been a schoolteacher for 25 years. When she heard about a job that would mean a promotion, she applied for the position. However, someone who had been teaching for only one year was hired instead. She went to the principal and asked why. The principal responded, "I'm sorry, but you haven't had 25 years of experience as you claim; you've had only one year's experience 25 times." During that whole time the teacher had not improved.

John 15:16 (KJV) *Ye have not chosen me, but I have chosen you, and ordained you, that ye should go and bring forth fruit, and that your fruit should remain: that whatsoever ye shall ask of the Father in my name, he may give it you.*

I remember what it felt like when I was offered the position as a Special Education Teacher. I was so proud and thankful for the opportunity to teach school, to impart some of the knowledge God allowed me to obtain with others. I believe there are four kinds of people, those who do not do the job they have been hired to do, those who go through the motion and do as little as they can, those who fulfill their mission, and those who think, they can make the world they live in a better place. Each of us falls into one of these categories: Those who bear no fruit, those who bear fruit, those who bear more fruit and those who bear much fruit. Either, you are un-fruitful or fruitful. No matter where you find yourself, prayer is the answer.

PRAYER
✼✼✼✼✼✼

Thank you oh Lord for this beautiful day. Lord thank you for your goodness to me and my family. Lord I fall short so many times, but you still love me, and call me your child. I love you so much; Lord no matter my condition you still embrace me with your unconditional Love, grace and mercy. Father in the name of Jesus, I come to you with an open mind, and open heart and thanks giving on my lips. Dear Lord create in me a clean and pure heart and renew a right Spirit within me. Lord I understand, that only what I do for you will last. Thank you for Father for loving me, and accepting me. I realize I am nothing without you. Lord I desire a touch from you, and I need you every moment of each day. Lord continue to strengthen me where I am weak. Lord help me to be fruitful in all that I do. Lord in all I do let it bring you honor and glory. In Jesus mighty name, Amen

THE TRUST FACTOR

I was told at a very young age that your word is your bond. In other words, if you commit to doing something, do what you say. My Dad said to me once, "You are as good as your word". If you are employed, I am certain that you expect to be compensated. you anticipate a salary from your employer. Most of us have direct deposit, and we trust the date our monies will be available to us. When our physician gives us a prescription and we take it to our pharmacy, we trust that we are getting what our physician has prescribed. Most of the people we trust, we have a lucrative relationship with them. Trust is the firmest building block in human relationships. Without trust, the whole structure comes falling down. Trustworthiness is a highly esteem commodity. If you are trustworthy it is considered valuable.

Genesis 20: 11-13 (KJV) *[11] And Abraham said, because I thought, surely the fear of God is not in this place; and they will slay me for my wife's sake. [12] And yet indeed she is my sister; she is the daughter of my father, but not the daughter of my mother; and she became my wife. [13] And it came to pass, when God caused me to wander from my father's house, that I said unto her, This is thy kindness which thou shalt shew unto me; at every place whither we shall come, say of me, He is my brother.*

Because Abraham mistakenly assumed that Abimelech was a wicked man, he made a quick decision to tell a half-truth. Abraham thought it would be more effective to deceive Abimelech than to trust God to work in the King's life. Don't assume that God will not work in a situation that has potential problems. You may completely understand the situation, and God may intervene when you least expect it. Doing the impossible is everyday business for God. Our big problems may not seem so impossible if we let God handle them. We sometimes act as if we know more about our situations than

God does; He is the one who made us and has foreseen the problem beforehand.

Proverbs 3:5-6 (KJV) *5Trust in the Lord with all thine heart; and lean not unto thine own understanding. 6In all thy ways acknowledge him, and he shall direct thy paths.*

We must remember God is omnipotent; He is everywhere at the same time. Our vision is limited, and we cannot out smart our creator. He has done more than any human being is capable of for His children, and we still sometimes doubt His word.

Micah 7:5-6 (KJV) *5Trust ye not in a friend, put ye not confidence in a guide: keep the doors of thy mouth from her that lieth in thy bosom. 6For the son dishonored the father, the daughter riseth up against her mother, the daughter in law against her mother in law; a man's enemies are the men of his own house.*

We all have been guilty of trusting people more that our Heavenly Father. I believe that some of us have been extremely hurt by people that we choose to trust the most. I thank God that He will never hurt us or portray His children. His desire is to love us and take perfect care of us.

According to **Deuteronomy 28:12-13 (KJV)** *12The Lord shall open unto thee his good treasure, the heaven to give the rain unto thy land in his season, and to bless all the work of thine hand: and thou shalt lend unto many nations, and thou shalt not borrow. 13And the Lord shall make thee the head, and not the tail; and thou shalt be above only, and thou shalt not be beneath; if that thou hearken unto the commandments of the Lord thy God, which I command thee this day, to observe and to do them.*

If we trust God, His blessing will chase us down. **Psalm 1:1-5 (KJV)** *1Blessed is the man that walketh not in the counsel of the ungodly, nor standeth in the way of sinners, nor sitteth in the seat of the scornful. 2But his delight is in the law of the LORD; and in his law doth* *he meditate day and night. ³And he shall be like a tree planted by the rivers of water, that bringeth forth his fruit in his season; his leaf also shall not wither; and whatsoever he doeth shall prosper. ⁴The ungodly are not so: but are like the chaff which the wind driveth away. ⁵Therefore the ungodly shall not stand in the judgment, nor sinners in the congregation of the righteous.*

Because we love God and desire to do His will, He will give us the desires of our heart. We are not perfect by any means, but we have a heart for our Lord and Savior Jesus Christ. We as Christians want to please God when we diligently seek Him with all our heart. He will not disappoint us.

PRAYER
✱✱✱✱✱

Dear God, thank you for your awesomeness. Thank you for being the Father that you are to your children. Lord, I believe you are delighted when your children come to you. Today, Oh Lord, I come to you not asking for anything, but to say thank you Lord for looking beyond my faults and seeing my need. Father, teach us how to pray and what to pray for. Lord, I realize that trust doesn't come easy for some; but Lord help us to trust in you and you alone. Lord, our hope is built on nothing less than Jesus' blood and righteousness. Know that God loves you and wants to bless you. Father, bless everyone praying this prayer. Help them put their trust in you, the giver of life. In Jesus' precious name, we pray. Amen.

Patricia S. Quillen

A PINK TORNADO

During my interview for my current job, one of the questions I was asked by the interviewer was, "are you apart of a click"? My response was, "No I am not. I applied for this vacancy because I am a well-rounded, people-person. I love people; I need a job; and I have a strong desire to work in my field of study." That was my answer. I believe the world is filled with two- faced people and people that are not real. The world has more than enough people that play games and gossip.

Ephesians 4:29 (NIV) Let no corrupt communication proceed out of your mouth, but that which is good to the use of edifying, that it may minister grace unto the hearers.

I believe one of the reasons some people gossip is because they desire to appear to make themselves look better in the eyes of others and they put others down to accomplish this goal. A person that gossips is dangerous, not only to others, but to themselves. I was told as a child, "If you cannot say anything positive about a person, do not say anything at all."

Proverbs 20:19 (ESV) Whoever goes about slandering reveals secrets; therefore do not associate with a simple babbler.

Proverbs 26:20 (KJV) Where no wood is, there the fire goeth out: so where there is no talebearer, the strife ceaseth.

When we speak negatively about others, we destroy their character and credibility, and it does not do anything for us. We all have been guilty of fault finding, judging others, and saying things that are not good and in poor taste. We should desire to seek God's guidance and wisdom when we are faced with the opportunity to lift others up or the choice to tear others down. People will confess to many others sins but very few will admit to gossiping. Gossip causes division, hurt, and animosity between family and friends. Gossip can tear down in a second what it took years to build. God's Word tells us that our words to other people can bring life or they can bring death.

According to ***James 3:5-6 (KJV)*** *⁵Even so the tongue is a little member, and boasteth great things. Behold, how great a matter a little fire kindleth! ⁶And the tongue is a fire, a world of iniquity: so is the tongue among our members, that it defileth the whole body, and setteth on fire the course of nature; and it is set on fire of hell.*

Let your words be few. Encourage others with the word of God. Treat others the way you want others to treat you. Positive words encourages a positive attitude. Remember the old saying "what goes around comes back around." A tree is known by the fruit it bears, bitter or sweet.

Proverbs 6: 16-19 (KJV) *¹⁶These six things doth the Lord hate: yea, seven are an abomination unto him: ¹⁷A proud look, a lying tongue, and hands that shed innocent blood, ¹⁸An heart that deviseth wicked imaginations, feet that be swift in running to mischief, ¹⁹A false witness that speaketh lies, and he that soweth discord among brethren.*

In all that we do, seek peace and show others the love of God.

PRAYER
✳✳✳✳✳✳

Oh, mighty God, thank you for your grace. Lord, there have been times we have all been guilty for speaking negatively of others. Lord, help us to keep our minds on you and your ways. Lord, help us to put on the breast plate of righteousness. Lord help us to remember the same measure we use against others, that same measure will be used against us. Father you are a God of love and not confusion, help us to focus on you and your goodness. Lord help us to pray more for our brothers and sisters. Lord we all fall short and none is perfect but you. Lord, our desire is to please you. Lord, we want our life to represent you. Father, you are our role model when others look at us. Allow them to see you in our character and actions. These precious blessings we ask in your name. Amen.

Chapter 9

PEACE BE STILL

People that know me, know that I am an easy-going person. I try to keep peace at all times. In my immediate family, I am known as the peace maker. I believe Christians are sometimes mistreated, because we tried to live a Godly lifestyle by doing what is right. There is an old saying, "hurting people hurt people". Often, people that hurt other people are experiencing pain, a hurt with unresolved issues in their life. Our flesh will say, "I have nothing to do with what they are going through", and we want to retaliate. However, the God on the inside of us as Christians, must be Bigger than our feelings. Feelings come and go.

2 Corinthians 4:8-12 (NKJV) is telling us Christians that *[8]We are hard-pressed on every side, yet not crushed; we are perplexed, but not in despair; [9]persecuted, but not forsaken; struck down, but not destroyed—[10]always carrying about in the body the dying of the Lord Jesus, that the life of Jesus also may be manifested in our body. [11]For we who live are always* delivered to death for Jesus' sake, that the life of Jesus also may be manifested in our mortal flesh. ^{12}So then death is working in us, but life in you.

When you are hard pressed in your world of effort, the vital thing to do is move forward rather than to despair and be crushed. Press into what is difficult, use all the abilities God provided you, and become resilient as a result of the experience.

Ephesians 4:26-31 (NKJV) ^{26}*Be angry, and do not sin, do not let the sun go down on your wrath, ^{27}nor give place to the devil. 28Let him who stole steal no longer, but rather let him labor, working with his hands what is good, that he may have something to give him who has need. ^{29}Let no corrupt word proceed out of your mouth, but what is good for necessary edification, that it may impart grace to the hearers. ^{30}And do not grieve the Holy Spirit of God, by whom you were sealed for the day of redemption. ^{31}Let all bitterness, wrath, anger, clamor, and evil speaking be put away from you, with all malice.*

When you find that you are angry and upset with another person, pray first and ask the Lord for His guidance. When we say things in anger, we are often sorry later, however once those words come from our lips, we can never take them back. Remember our words have power, positive or negative. According to **James 1:19-20 (NKJV)** *^{19}So then, my beloved brethren, let every man be swift to hear, slow to speak, slow to wrath; ^{20}for the wrath of man does not produce the righteousness of God.* My dear brothers and sisters take note that the battle is not yours! It is the Lord's. However, prayer is essential before making any decision. Seek the help of the Holy Spirit. Peace and fullness of love will not be activated unless we replace our anger with a loving spirit.

Proverbs 29:22 (NKJV) *An angry man stirs up strife, And a furious man abounds in transgression.*

Proverbs 29:11 (NLT) *Fools vent their anger, but the wise quietly hold it back.*

As a Christian, the controlling of your anger is the fruit of the Holy Spirit's work in your life.

2 Corinthians 10:3-5 (NIV) *³For though we live in the world, we do not wage war as the world does. ⁴The weapons we fight with are not the weapons of the world. On the contrary, they have divine power to demolish strongholds. ⁵We demolish arguments and every pretension that sets itself up against the knowledge of God, and we take captive every thought to make it obedient to Christ.*

Proverbs 14: 29 (NLT) *People with understanding control their anger; a hot temper shows great foolishness."*

1 Corinthians 13:4-8 (NLT) *⁴Love is patient and kind. Love is not jealous or boastful or proud ⁵or rude. It does not demand its own way. It is not irritable, and it keeps no record of being wronged. ⁶It does not rejoice about injustice but rejoices whenever the truth wins out. ⁷Love never gives up, never loses faith, is always hopeful, and endures through every circumstance. ⁸Prophecy and speaking in unknown languages and special knowledge will become useless. But love will last forever!*

These are the attributes of our God. Sometimes we are justified when we get upset with others, because we were mistreated; however, in other cases from my experience, the reasons we get angry is because of identified flaws within ourselves that we have not allow the Holy Spirit to change. Ask God for His divine intervention. After we have stripped away our anger, only then can we finally put on love and self-control. Without stripping out the root cause of our anger, it is like putting a coat of paint on a dirty wall, and hoping that it will stick. Afterwards, real healing can come when we affirm our purpose of living to do God's will, to exert self-control and to love one another. "Challenges are what make life interesting and overcoming them is what makes life meaningful."

PRAYER

Father, this is a day that you have made, and I will rejoice and be glad in it. Thank you, Lord, for peace beyond human understanding. Thank you, Lord, for your daily benefits. Father, when I think of your goodness and all that you have done for me, my soul cries out thank you, Jesus. I thank you, Lord, for every opportunity to praise your Holy and righteous name. Father, continue to shower them with your Holy Spirit. No matter what we may be facing today, help us understand the battle is not ours, but yours. Lord help our lives to represent the fruit of the Spirit. Lord your word clearly tells us get angry, but sin not. you are our vindicator, refuge and strength. In Jesus' powerful and mighty name, we pray these blessings, Amen.

LORD, HELP MY UNBELIEF

Doubt is something every person has experienced at some point, yet something that we do not always handle well. ***James 1: 5-8 (KJV)*** *⁵If any of you lack wisdom, let him ask of God, that giveth to all men liberally, and upbraideth not; and it shall be given him. ⁶But let him ask in faith, nothing wavering. ⁷For he that wavereth is like a wave of the sea driven with the wind and tossed. For let not that man think that he shall receive any thing of the Lord. ⁸A double minded man is unstable in* *all his ways.* Faith and doubt are opposites. I can remember praying and not believing in my heart that God was going to answer my prayer. There have been times that I would pray and then my mind would wander in doubt for one reason or another. I have found it helpful to read scripture pertaining to my circumstance, and say what God's Word says about my situation. I believe God, even when I cannot see how He is going to work in my situation. If I could see the outcome, it would not take faith. I believe God, because he is my Father and He cannot lie. His track record is impeccable. When I pray, I ask the Lord to conform my will and desire to His will and His desire for my life.

Genesis 12:1-4 (KJV) *¹Now the LORD had said unto Abram, Get thee out of thy country, and from thy kindred, and from thy father's house, unto a land that I will shew thee: ²And I will make of thee a great nation, and I will bless thee, and make thy name great; and thou shalt be a blessing: ³And I will bless them that bless thee, and curse him that curseth thee: and in thee shall all families of the earth be blessed. ⁴So Abram departed, as the LORD had spoken unto him; and Lot went with him: and Abram was seventy and five years old when he departed out of Haran.*

We do not understand everything God tells us to do. That is where faith comes in. God doesn't want instability in His children, nor does He want luke warm Christians.

Matthew 7:7(KJV) *Ask, and it shall be given you; seek, and ye shall find; knock, and it shall be opened unto you.* If we really believe God, we would stand on His Word.

Doubt eats away at our mind, like cancer eats away our body. So, it's only natural that our minds start to associate God with all of our other ultimate concerns, the ones that have failed us.

Consequently, we start to fear that He'll let us down too! That's why doubt comes so easily to us. When something unexpected happens, your spouse may ask for a divorce or you may lose your job or God doesn't heal your father's cancer. It seems obvious that the Lord is just one more ultimate concern unworthy of trust. We end up abandoning Him like all the other empty promises. Doubt is common: it happened repeatedly in the Bible! Remember when Peter stepped out of the boat to walk across the water and Jesus had to grab his arm to stop him from swimming with the fishes? Why? He doubted! Thomas, who hung around with Jesus for three years, refused to believe the Master rose again until he got to feel the nail-scarred hands. Jesus is incredibly merciful!

When everything seems lost, when God allows us to suffer and we wonder if He's there and whether we can trust Him, look back from where He brought you from. When you and I doubt God's Word, we distrust it without a cause. There has never been a time that I have called on my heavenly father and He was not there. We need to believe in what we ask for, because of who we are asking! Use the power of your creativity to help you see the options that are available to you and to help you open the doors that will lead you to the person you desire to be. Believe in God first; take Him at His word. Remember, the abilities He has placed on the inside of you, to create whatever you dream of deep in your heart. I challenge you; do not allow doubt or wavering in your faith to take residence in your head. When faced with doubt, think on where God has brought you, and focus on His word. We have a team of angelic helpers that are so honored to experience in our journey and welcome us into their embrace as they surround us with the loving light of their 'angel wings'. Know you are not alone.

Take the time to become quiet and reach for that stillness that lies within the void of silence and listen carefully for that is where you will find the promptings of your spirit-self, your angels, and your guides that are guiding, comforting, loving and supporting you.

❧ PRAYER ❧
✳✳✳✳✳✳

Father, I thank you for this new day fill with your sweet fragrance. Lord, I thank you for your grace and mercy. Father thank you for strength and power to do your will. Lord help your children to lean and depend upon you, not on material gain or other people. Lord, help us not to live a life of doubt and uncertainty; help us not to waver in our faith. Lord, we realize that doubt and unbelief will come, but give us the power to overcome. Lord, our ultimate desire is to trust in you and you alone. Lord conform our will to your will. Where there is doubt, help us to believe in you and your Holy Word. We serve an awesome God, the God that created us and the universe. Lord we want our lives to bring you glory and honor, these precious blessing we ask in your righteous name, Amen.

GOOGLE DOES NOT HAVE ALL THE ANSWERS

I have often felt out of place in the company of people I perceive to be more intelligent than me. I remember, as a novice teacher, being in the presence of veteran teachers that I felt inadequate to say the least. I felt I did not know anything about teaching compared to my peers. However, the Holy Spirit reminded me that I have taught others most of my adult life and not as a professional. Since that revelation, I do not compare myself to others. Without God's help, you will never become who you were meant to be. Once you know who you are, you can fit in anywhere.

2 Timothy 1:7 (KJV) *For God hath not given us the spirit of fear; but of power, and of love, and of a sound mind.*

We are all familiar with the story of Joseph. What the enemy meant for harm, God turned around for his good. Joseph had been betrayed by his brothers and sold to desert traders who took him to Egypt where they sold him to a man named Potiphar who was head of Pharaoh's security detail. Joseph is far from home, and he is a slave in Egypt. His brothers have abandoned him and his father thinks he's dead. Obviously, his future appears to be very bleak indeed. **Genesis 39:2-4(KJV)** *²And the Lord was with Joseph, and he was a prosperous man; and he was in the house of his master the Egyptian. ³And his master saw that the Lord was with him, and that the Lord made all that he did to prosper in his hand. ⁴And Joseph found grace in his sight, and he served him: and he made him overseer over his house, and all that he had he put into his hand.*

When his master saw that the Lord was with him and that the Lord gave him success in everything he did, Joseph found favor in his eyes and became his attendant. Potiphar put him in charge of his household and he entrusted to his care everything he owned. When we understand who Christ is in us, we can embrace who we are to God.

The reason some Christians are defeated is that they get their identity from the wrong places. As Christians, the reason that we lose so often when we battle temptation is because we don't know who we are. Everyone originally gets their sense of self, from their parents, caretakers and socicty. It's part of a process called socialization. We gain our sense of self from the way others view us. Lost people can spot a phony a mile away, and they can recognize God's hand at work in a believer's life. Potiphar may have followed a pagan religion, but he understood that Joseph was different, and he respected him for it. In my experience, people may disagree with you sometimes, but when you stand for what is right, they will respect you.

As believers, we can know we belong to God and that God defines who we are and what we are meant to do on this Earth. Trying to be someone God never intended you to be causes stress, anxiety, and self-humiliation! Know who you want to please. Jesus never let the fear of rejection manipulate him. No one can pressure you without your permission.

Luke 4:42–44 (KJV) *42And when it was day, he departed and went into a desert place: and the people sought him, and came unto him, and stayed him, that he should not depart from them. 43And he said unto them, I must preach the kingdom of God to other cities also: for therefore am I sent. 44And he preached in the synagogues of Galilee."*

John 10:10 (KJV) *The thief cometh not, but for to steal, and to kill, and to destroy: I am come that they might have life, and that they might have it more abundantly.*

PRAYER
✹✹✹✹✹

Father, thank you for another opportunity to praise your Holy name. Lord, thank you for being so good to me and my family. Lord, when my days are dark, and my eyes are filled with tears, I know that you are there. Lord, when I feel alone, I know you are forever near. Father, I know in you, I have life. In you, I have hope and your assurance that this too will pass. Lord, no day is a bad day. On days when I feel my strength is limited, I know in you there are no limits. Lord, bless everyone praying this prayer. Lord, encourage them. Lord, wrap your loving arms around them, and whisper to them, like only you can. The peace that passes all understanding is in you, Lord. Father, every answer can be found in your word. These precious blessings we ask in your name. Amen.

HOW BIG IS YOUR GOD?

I was thinking about how big our God is. I am still in awe of our God, my infinite mind cannot conceive the bigness of our heavenly father. Looking back on my life and the promises of God that He has fulfilled is astonishing. God is bigger than problems and anything seen or unseen. It is impossible to comprehend the immensity of God.

Isaiah 40: 12 (KJV) *Who hath measured the waters in the hollow of his hand, and meted out heaven with the span, and comprehended the dust of the earth in a measure, and weighed the mountains in scales, and the hills in a balance?*

1 Timothy 2:4-6 (KJV) *[4]Who will have all men to be saved, and to come unto the knowledge of the truth. [5]For there is one God, and one* *mediator between God and men, the man Christ Jesus; ⁶Who gave himself a ransom for all, to be testified in due time.*

2 Peter 3:9 (KJV) *The Lord is not slack concerning his promise, as some men count slackness; but is longsuffering to us-ward, not willing that any should perish, but that all should come to repentance.*

This great God who created all that is seen and unseen is the same God who cares for you and me with an unconditional and unwavering love. This God is the One "who desires all men to be saved and to come to the knowledge of the truth". God's desire is to have all of his precious children saved. He desires to abundantly bless us with His goodness. Often in the midst of hard times, struggles and disappointments we tend to feel all alone and think that God has forgotten us, but it is simply not true. God is always ready, willing and able to provide, but He expects faith and trust on our part.

Psalm 84:11 (KJV) *For the Lord God is a sun and shield: the Lord will give grace and glory: no good thing will he withhold from them that walk uprightly.*

Matthew 6:25 – 26(KJV) *²⁵Therefore I say unto you, Take no thought for your life, what ye shall eat, or what ye shall drink; nor yet for your body, what ye shall put on. Is not the life more than meat, and the body than raiment? ²⁶Behold the fowls of the air: for they sow not, neither do they reap, nor gather into barns; yet your heavenly Father feedeth them. Are ye not much better than they?*

Ephesians 2:10 (KJV) *For we are his workmanship, created in Christ Jesus unto good works, which God hath before ordained that we should walk in them.*

He who is in you is greater than he who is in the world. If God is for us, who can be against us? We are more than conquerors through Him who loved us." I want to challenge you to pray without ceasing and seek God while He may be found; there will come a time when we are unable to pray. We need to fill our store house with prayers. Life and death is in the power of what we say.

PRAYER

I can only imagine, when that day comes, to meet my Lord and Savior, how happy I will be! Just to be surrounded by His glory, I can only imagine. Lord thank you for being an ever present help in our time of need. Thank you for being an awesome Father, Counselor and Teacher to your children. Lord you are a very Big God, and we give you honor and praise, for all of your daily benefits. Father thank you for looking beyond our faults and seeing our needs. Lord we love you and honor you for the God that you are. Lord we desire your will to be our will. Lord, transform us, mold us and shape us into what you want us to be. Lord bless everyone praying this prayer. In Jesus precious name, Amen.

DILIGENCE IS A GOD THING

I've desired to become smaller. One thing I've chosen for a discipline is walking. So I started walking two miles a day.

When I first started, my breathing was rapid. I was short of breath and I wanted to stop, but I counted the cost of giving up verses being diligent to the end for my desired goal. So I persevered. I have to accomplish this and I am not a quitter. Of course, the enemy brought to my mind all times I attempted and failed in losing weight. ***Philippians 4:13*** *I can do all things through Christ that strengthens me.* The enemy is quick to remind us of our past failures and mistakes. Spending quality time with our Heavenly Father is essential to our spiritual well-being for it will build spiritual character, perseverance and endurance. Getting physically fit is important, our body is God's holy temple; but spiritual exercise is much more important and is a tonic for all you do. So exercise yourself spiritually, and practice being a better Christian.

According to ***2 Timothy 4:7-8 (KJV)*** *7I have fought a good fight, I have finished my course, I have kept the faith: 8Henceforth there is laid up for me a crown of righteousness, which the Lord, the righteous judge, shall give me at that day: and not to me only, but unto all them also that love his appearing.* Our life here is temporary, for those of us that are working for the Kingdom we have a reward waiting. The word of God tells us that one day our earthly house is going to decay.

Romans 8:37-39 (KJV) *37Nay in all these things we are more than conquerors through him that loved us. 38For I am persuaded, that neither death, nor life, nor angels, nor principalities, nor powers, nor things present, nor things to come, 39Nor height, nor depth, nor any other creature, shall be able to separate us from the love of God, which is in Christ Jesus our Lord."*

President Henry B. Eying, first counselor in the First

Presidency, spoke about diligence and explained how there is a pattern needed to be diligent servants of God. He gave a list of four things to be done, which are: Learn what the Lord expects of you, Make a plan to do it, Act on your plan with diligence, Share with others how your experience changed you and blessed others.

Hebrews 11:6 (KJV) *But without faith it is impossible to please Him, for he who comes to God must believe that He is, and that He is a rewarder of those who diligently seek Him.*

According to **Ephesians 5:1-2 (KJV)** *¹Be ye therefore followers of God, as dear children; ²And walk in love, as Christ also hath loved us, and hath given himself for us an offering and a sacrifice to God for a sweet-smelling savour.*

Numbers 23:19-20 (KJV) *¹⁹God is not a man that he should lie; neither the son of man that he should repent: hath he said, and shall he not do it? or hath he spoken, and shall he not make it good? ²⁰Behold, I have received commandment to bless: and he hath blessed; and I cannot reverse it.*

God is no freeloader and can be counted on 100 percent of the time. He wants His children to be imitators of Him, He set up the principles of sowing and reaping and the law of giving and receiving.

Proverbs 21:5 (KJV) *The thoughts of the diligent tend only to plenteousness; but of every one that is hasty only to want.* Planning includes praying thinking and preparing. In contrast, someone who doesn't take the time to think things through, or adequately prepare, wastes time and effort.

Proverbs 13:4 (KJV) *The soul of the sluggard desireth, and hath* *nothing: but the soul of the diligent shall be made fat."*

PRAYER
✻✻✻✻✻

Father in the name of Jesus, thank you for this awesome day. Thank you for your goodness, and blessings that you have bestowed upon me. Lord my desire is to please you and walk in integrity. Lord thank you for your faithfulness. Lord, you are my strength and my shield; I give you praise and honor. Father help us to be diligent in all we do and enlarge our territory. Lord transform our will to your will. Lord we desire to please you, and bring you honor. Lord give us the strength and perseverance to do your will. Lord give your children boldness to declare your name, In Jesus mighty name, Amen.

CHAPTER 10

FULFILL YOUR MINISTRY

When the Lord called me into the ministry, I searched His Word, because I desired to be obedient and sure of His will for my life. As I began to search the scriptures, God reiterated to me what I heard Him say to me in His audible voice. God does not have a problem speaking to us, but sometimes we have a problem hearing Him. When God gives us a word, He is very clear and concise. Part of my directions can be found in **2 Timothy 4:3-5 (KJV)** *³For the time will come when they will not endure sound doctrine; but after their own lusts shall they heap to themselves teachers, having itching ears; ⁴And they shall turn away their ears from the truth, and shall be turned unto fables. ⁵But watch thou in all things, endure afflictions, do the work of an evangelist, make full proof of thy ministry.*

If you are seeking directions because you are not sure of your calling, continue to pray and admit to God the place that you are in. God's desire is to make Himself clear to you. Confusion comes from the enemy; it is the enemies desire to keep us in doubt. As Christians, we want to do what God wants so we can really stress over discerning His call on our lives. As we are all called to work in the natural, we also have a work to do in the spiritual. Jesus was the son of God and worked as a carpenter. **Matthew 13:55 (KJV)** *Is not this the carpenter's son? Is not his mother called Mary? And are not his brothers James and Joseph and Simon and Judas?* But today, we have the opportunity to do almost anything.

In the past, people have asked me what it felt like to receive a call from God to be an evangelist. My response has always been, "It's an honor."

When God speaks; listen. When God gives directions follow His divine plan. People I trust have helped me tremendously, to assess my strengths and weaknesses. People have also prayed for me. God repeated what He spoke to me. I pray to God daily expressing how much I long to be in His will. I always knew there was a call on my life. I was not altogether sure to what to expect until the commitment level was raised. Then He took control. God is my everything and we all can trust God. Our Heavenly Father gave each of us a mind to reflect the rationality in us; God will never circumvent our will nor understandings. He wants our decision-making to image Him. Actually, that means we can't turn our minds off and expect the Holy Spirit to take over. God is sovereign over the tiniest details of our lives. We know He will lead us even if He doesn't tell us where exactly we're going. He made us, calls us, and will guide us to exactly the place He wants us.

Psalm 40:8 (Holman Christian Bible) *I delight to do your will, my God; your instruction resides within me.* I get so much pleasure walking in my calling. I am thankful that God chose me for such a time as this. I love the Lord because He first loved me. God is an awesome father to His children. His love and devotion is never contingent on our obedience. I have learned the more time you spend in his word, the more you will long to please Him and live your life to honor Him. I challenge you to get to know God and your life will never be the same. Expect God to do something wonderful in your life today.

God in His infinite wisdom created us in His image, we are His masterpiece, therefore we are to be like Him. Our attitudes and behavior should represent Him at all times. Be mindful of how you speak and act, because someone is watching you. Do they desire to have what you are displaying? ***Psalm 138:8 (KJV)*** *The Lord will perfect that which concerns me; your mercy, O Lord, endures forever; Do not forsake the works of your hands.*

✥PRAYER✥
✱✱✱✱✱

Father, thank you for your goodness, grace and mercy. Lord, thank you for not giving me what I deserve. Thank you for your love, patience and guidance. Lord, thank you for the mind to serve you and the mind to want to please you. Lord, as I think of your goodness and from where you brought me, I am still amazed that you love me so much. Lord let my light so shine that others will see you in me. Father, I honor and adore you. Lord for the ones that maybe struggling with doubt, disappointment, depression and loneliness be their help. Lord give them direction and your wisdom. Lord help us to walk with our heads held high and speak boldly of your goodness. Father give us clarity and understanding in all that concerns you, In Jesus mighty name, Amen.

Be silent before the Lord, and wait expectantly on Him.
Psalm 37:7

THIS PLACE

There is a similar yet different place in each of our lives. We all have experienced this place, and if you have not, wait a while. There is a true familiar saying, "There has to be some rain in your life, to appreciate the sunshine". This place may be feeling overwhelmed, lacking in finances, losing a job, having marital issues, or disobeying, unruly children. I thought, at one time, God only gave revelation to individuals that appeared to have their lives in order. However, because of my limited knowledge of God's Word, I was deceived. Thank God for His revelation.

2 Timothy 2:15 (KJV) *Study to shew thyself approved unto God, a workman that needeth not to be ashamed, rightly dividing the word of truth."* At one time I was asked the Lord to use me, but at this point in my life, I am asking the Lord to make me usable.

According to ***James 5:17(KJV)*** *Elias was a man subject to like passions as we are, and he prayed earnestly that it might not rain: and it rained not on the earth by the space of three years and six months.*
This reference is talking about the time Elijah became so despondent that he asked God to kill him. Elijah wasn't perfect; yet, he called fire down from heaven three times; he was the first person to raise someone from the dead; he caused the greatest revival in history up to that point; his word started and ended a three-year drought; and he multiplied food in a miraculous way.

There is a lot we can learn from a man like this, both positive and negative. God uses ordinary people like you and me to fulfill His purpose. The Bible gives little background on Elijah. It wasn't his pedigree or education that brought him into a position of influence and power. Elijah was nobody until he received a word from God. It was the revelation God gave him that put him into a position of leadership. Likewise, anyone who is born again, baptized in the Holy Spirit, or has a good relationship with the Lord can receive revelation from God too. Just as Elijah's revelation from God put him into a position of influence, anyone who has a revelation of God has the potential to influence others also. Elijah became the most sought after man in the nation. God said "your gift will make room for you. Allow the Heavenly Father to order your steps.

Proverbs 18:16 (KJV) *A man's gift maketh room for him, and bringeth him before great men.*

1 Kings 17:2-4(KJV) *And the word of the Lord came unto him, saying, Get thee hence, and turn thee eastward, and hide thyself by the brook Cherith, that is before Jordan. And it shall be, that thou shalt drink of the brook; and I have commanded the ravens to feed thee there.* God doesn't reveal His complete plan to us immediately, nor does He reveal his entire plan to us all at once. He reveals His plan to us one step at a time. We must be willing to go and do what God says.

After we obey the first step, He shows us the next. Don't try to figure out the next step until you have acted on what you know to do now. Elijah's miracle wasn't where he was but where the Lord was sending him. Each of us has a place where the blessings of the Lord are waiting. We must ask the Lord to give us a discerning ear to hear Him and clarity to understand His instructions. The Lord never fails to provide, but we often fail to receive, because of our lack of knowledge, and our disobedience.

PRAYER

Lord, thank you for your provision. Thank you Lord for your grace and your mercy. Lord, you are an awesome Father to your children. Lord, sometimes when we are going through a challenging season, we tend not to hear your voice or your instruction. Lord, there have been times in my life when I did not understand your plan, and I went contrary to your will. Lord, I thank you for your compassion and your unconditional love for me. Lord open our minds and give us your understanding. Lord, thank you for being a wonderful father; we love you and adore you. Lord even when we find ourselves in this place we will trust you. Lord, your Word will never fail, we know that faith comes by hearing. Lord, help us to increase our faith more and spend more time in prayer and in your word. Lord, bless everyone praying this prayer. Continue to give us revelation into the things that concern you. In Jesus' precious name, we pray. Amen.

OBEDIENCE IS BETTER THAN A SACRIFICE

My definition of God's blessing is any expression of God's goodness and love toward us; however, God sometimes chooses to bless us in other ways. For example, He grants us strength, peace and joy in the midst of hardship, and He uses our suffering to help us mature spiritually.

2 Corinthians 11:22 (KJV) *Are they Hebrews? so am I. Are they Israelites? So am I. Are they the seed of Abraham? So am I.*

He has also sealed us and given us the Spirit as a down compensation in our hearts. Paul obeyed God by preaching the gospel. As a result, he suffered tremendous persecution, danger, and physical abuse. However, because he was imprisoned, the apostle had time to write his epistles to the Colossians, Philippians, Ephesians, and Philemon. His obedience resulted in a supernatural blessing. Often, the first effect of obedience is not blessing, but suffering. Sometimes, what God requires of us will initially lead to pain and sadness. We shouldn't assume that difficulty means we've made a mistake or that He has abandoned us. Obedience is a choice and a lifestyle.

Sometimes, I believe God allows us to suffer in order to bring us to the end of ourselves. We become most useful to the Lord when we rely on Him completely. If we respond correctly to loss and suffering, we will find blessing through it. Although suffering does not feel good to our flesh, embrace it, because there is a reward when we come through it. We must pass the test. Also, suffering reminds us that all good things are gifts from God and not earned by our own efforts. In suffering, you and I have the opportunity to become living examples of the goodness of God. As others watch how we respond to overwhelming adversity, they recognize His loving care. When we obey God, we can expect His blessings to overtake us. But remember that His choice of blessing may be different from ours. Perhaps He will use suffering to draw us closer to Him;

or He may use it to remove from our life those things that hinder fruitfulness for Him. Nonetheless, if you walk in His will, He will bless you in unimaginable and incomprehensible ways.

Deuteronomy 28:1-4 (Authorized KJV) *1And it shall come to pass, if thou shalt hearken diligently unto the voice of the Lord thy God, to observe and to do all his commandments which I command thee this day, that the Lord thy God will set thee on high above all nations of the earth: 2And all these blessings shall come on thee, and overtake thee, if thou shalt hearken unto the voice of the Lord thy God. 3Blessed shalt thou be in the city, and blessed shalt thou be in the field. 4Blessed shall be the fruit of thy body, and the fruit of thy ground, and the fruit of thy cattle, the increase of thy kine, and the flocks of thy sheep.*

Ephesians 6:5-9 (ESV) *5Slaves, obey your earthly masters with fear and trembling, with a sincere heart, as you would Christ, 6not by the way of eye-service, as people-pleasers, but as servants of Christ, doing the will of God from the heart, 7rendering service with a good will as to the Lord and not to man, 8knowing that whatever good anyone does, this he will receive back from the Lord, whether he is a slave or free. 9Masters, do the same to them, and stop your threatening, knowing that he who is both their Master and yours is in heaven, and that there is no partiality with him.*

PRAYER
✹✹✹✹✹

Lord this is a day that you have orchestrated for such a time as this. I want to give you honor and praise that is due your name. Father, thank you for loving me, providing for me and never letting me go. Lord, I cannot thank you enough for your blessings, mercies and grace. Thank you, Jesus, for all *that you have given to my family and me to enjoy. Lord, we know that obedience is better than a sacrifice. Lord continue to give me understanding and clarity concerning your word and your will for my life. Lord, teach me how to depend more on you and less on my abilities. Lord, bless your children in abundance, in order for us to be a blessing to others. Father when others look at us, let them see you and your favor on our lives. Thank you Lord for strength to do your will. Lord you said ask and it shall be given, seek and ye shall find, knock and the door will be open. Father thank you for being so kind and patient with your children. Father we all fall from time to time, but thank you Lord for your daily forgiveness. Lord continue to shape us and mold us into what you desire us to be, All these blessings we ask humbly in your name. Amen*

A CLUTTERED MIND

Sometimes, my mind goes into so many different directions that it is difficult to get much accomplished. I have to make a conscience decision to focus and pray every day. I have to ask the Lord to help me and to keep my mind on Him and His Word. There are so many other things that are competing for our time, and our mind. In some instances, the things that clutter our minds are not always positive. Have you ever sat in church and your mind drifts off on other things? I know for a fact I have!

Isaiah 26:3 *Thou wilt keep him in perfect peace, whose mind is stayed on thee: because he trusteth in thee.* At any time, one's mind could go off into a tangent. When one has a cluttered mind, he comes to church and or Bible study, and while the word is being delivered his mind wonders with questions: "Can I do this? Should I be? Did I cut the stove off before leaving home?" "What am I cooking today for dinner?" "What am I going to do tomorrow?" "How can I get more organized?" or "When will I get a raise?" On an on with distractions, this is the battle of the mind.

Romans 8:6 (KJV) *For to be carnally minded is death; but to be spiritually minded is life and peace.* The cluttered mind is full of yesterdays, todays and tomorrows; a cluttered mind focuses on things, people and situations. Tremendous thorn brushes of worldly worries suffocate the Word of God. The enemy overwhelms us with so many things that there appears to be no room for God. It becomes difficult for us to hear when our minds are so cluttered with other things when God does indeed speak to our hearts. According to ***Ecclesiastes 3:8(KJV)*** *A time to love, and a time to hate; a time of war, and a time of peace.*

When your mind begins to wander, first, start praising God through thanksgiving and through acknowledging His character and attributes. This is one of the best ways I know to break the bonds of a wandering mind. Also, get a song in your heart and begin to sing. ***John 14:27 (KLJV)*** *says, "Peace I leave with you; my peace I give to you. Not as the world gives do I give to you. Let not your hearts be troubled, neither let them be afraid."* Second, we must commit by faith to resist outside clutter; we must be willing to evaluate our lives in the light of what we hear. It is spiritually impossible to apply the Word week after week and remain the same. As listeners, with committed minds, we become productive, maturing children of God.

Psalm 84:5 *Blessed is the man whose strength is in thee; in whose heart are the ways of them.* Lord there is so much competing for our time and attention, it is easy to allow our minds to wonder. Lord you said in your word that if we keep our minds on you, you will keep us in perfect peace.

Matthew 6:24 *No man can serve two masters: for either he will hate the one, and love the other; or else he will hold to the one, and despise the other. Ye cannot serve God and mammon.*

I challenge you to take your mind off the cares and worries of this world, everything will fail but the word of God. Trouble will not last forever.

Jonah2:7(KJV) *When my soul fainted within me I remembered the LORD: and my prayer came in unto thee, into thine holy temple.* When Jonah was in the belly of the whale, he made a conscience decision to take his mind off his trouble and focus on God.

2 Peter 3:17-18(KJV) *Ye therefore, beloved, seeing ye know these things before, beware lest ye also, being led away with the error of the wicked, fall from your own steadfastness. But grow in grace, and in the knowledge of our Lord and Savior Jesus Christ. To him be glory both now and forever. Amen.*

❧ PRAYER ❧

✸✸✸✸✸

Father, thank you for your awesome goodness and blessings that you shower your children with. Lord help us to focus on you and the things that concern you. Thank you, Lord, for giving me the mind and desire to live for you. Lord I am a continued work in progress and need you every day. Lord thank you for being the best father I could have. Lord, thank you for your peace, love and grace that you give to your children. Lord, there are so many things competing for our time and attention. Lord, we can rely on you and your Word to help us stay focused on you; and the things that bring you honor. Lord we love you and honor you in your Holy name, Amen.

THE OLD IS FAMILIAR BUT NEW IS BETTER

A few days ago, I was preparing to fried chicken for dinner. I had some old cooking oil and I added some new oil to the old. When the chicken was done it did not taste as fresh as I would have liked nor was the appearance appealing to me. Of course, it was edible, but I knew it could have tasted better and be more appealing to the eyes. That's the way some of our lives are; God is trying to do a new thing and we settle for less than His best. We are satisfied with the old, because it is familiar and comfortable. We have gotten use to the way things is and we are reluctant to change.

Matthew 9:17 *Neither do men put new wine into old bottles: else the bottles break, and the wine runneth out, and the bottles perish: but they put new wine into new bottles, and both are preserved.*

I believe when we desire God to do something new in our lives, we must be willing for Him to peel off the old layers for our newness to surface. Once a time ago, I had an apple. I was about to throw it away because of its appearance. From the outer appearance, it looked rotten. However after I peeled off the skin, the apple wasn't rotten after all; and that last bite was just as good as the first. It tasted delicious through and through. I would have missed a great moment of an edible pleasure. As the old saying goes, "We cannot always judge the book by its cover."

Ephesians 4:24(KJV) *And that ye put on the new man, which after God is created in righteousness and true holiness.*

Luke 5:36(KJV) *And he spake also a parable unto them; No man putteth a piece of a new garment upon an old; if otherwise, then both the new maketh a rent, and the piece that was taken out of the new agreeth not with the old.* When we accept Christ in our hearts, we become a new creature, old things are passed away; meaning our minds has to change. The enemy attacks the mind and thoughts. Have you ever for no apparent reason allowed your mind to wonder off, and then say to yourself, where did that thought come from? I was told as a child, an idle mind is the devil's playground. We can control what we entertain; in other words what we choose to enter our psyche. God has given us self-control, but we must choose to exercise it. You know how it is when you attempt to exercise and use muscles that you have not used in a while, they are stiff and they become sore. But the more you use them the less pain you will have to endure. When God saves our lives from the hand of the enemy, we begin to learn God's ways and His character, it changes us from the inside out. We mature. ***Luke 5:37-38 (KJV)*** *And no man putteth new wine into old bottles; else the new wine will burst the bottles, and be spilled, and the bottles shall perish. But new wine must be put into new bottles; and both are preserved.*

In putting on the new man, if we allow God will take away the spirit of Anger, wrath, malice, blasphemy, lying, backbiting, envy, jealous, and disobedience...... ***James 1:26 (KJV)*** *If any man among you seem to be religious, and bridleth not his tongue, but deceiveth his own heart, this man's religion is vain.* The tongue no man can tame, only God. When it comes to the ridding the old man and putting on the new one, it is certain they don't match. We cannot "mix and match." It is impossible to serve two masters. ***Matthew 6:24 (KJV)*** *No man can serve two masters: for either he will hate the one, and love the other; or else he will hold to the one, and despise the other. Ye cannot serve God and mammon.* We can think Godly thoughts, we can have Godly conversations. Be mindful of the things you listen to and the company you keep. ***I Corinthians 16:33*** *Do not be deceived: "Bad company ruins good morals."*

⁂ PRAYER ⁂
✸✸✸✸✸

Father in the name of Jesus, thank you for this new day filled with your awesome aroma. Thank you Lord for your mercy, grace and peace. Lord, although you see everything, I appreciate you for seeing me in the future and not hold my past and my present state against me. Thank you Lord for friends and family. Thank you Lord for connecting me with Godly advisors and praying people. Lord my deepest desire is to please you. Lord thank you for loving me, protecting me and investing in me. Lord I can never re-pay all that you have done and still doing in my life, but Lord I thank you! Thank you Lord for the doors that you are opening in my life. Lord I give you all praise and all the glory. Lord new is always better when we are in your hands. Lord you make us new and complete. and we are beautiful and wonderfully made. Lord your word says everything you made was good, and you made us in your image. Lord our desire is for you to take off the old and make us new in you. These precious blessings we ask in your Holy name, Amen.

Chapter 11

~~~

PRAYER FOR SPIRITUAL INSIGHT

One of things I desire from God is more Spiritual Insight. Spiritual Insight means "to distinguish, to separate out by diligent search, to examine." Discernment is the ability to properly discriminate or make determinations. It is actually related to wisdom. The Word of God itself is said to discern the thoughts and intentions of one's heart.

Hebrews 4:12 (KJV) *For the word of God is quick, and powerful, and sharper than any two-edged sword, piercing even to the dividing asunder of soul and spirit, and of the joints and marrow, and is a discerner of the thoughts and intents of the heart.*

1 Kings 3:9-11 (NKJV) *⁹Give therefore thy servant an understanding heart to judge thy people that I may discern between good and bad: for who is able to judge this thy so great a people. ¹⁰And the speech pleased the Lord, that Solomon had asked this thing. ¹¹And God said unto him, Because thou hast asked this thing, and hast not asked for thyself long life; neither hast asked riches for thyself, nor hast asked the life of thine enemies; but hast asked for thyself understanding to discern judgment;*

Proverbs 8:8-9 (KJV) *⁸All the words of my mouth are in righteousness; there is nothing froward or perverse in them. ⁹They are all plain to him that understandeth, and right to them that find knowledge.* God will give us insight into his Word, but we must study to show proof. When I was in school, our professor would lecture and I would take notes. If my class met two times a week for five hours, I would spend twice as much time out side of class to prepare for my exam. There is a price for God's anointing. If we desire the blessings God has for us and want a deeper relationship with Him, we must spend quality time with Him.

Romans 12:9 (NKJV), *says, Let love be without hypocrisy. Abhor what is evil. Cling to what is good.* Unless we have true discernment, we can't determine what is "evil" and what is "good" In order to maintain the gospel, the church, we must distinguish truth from dissent. Wisdom also demands that we accurately distinguish between what is "paramount" and what is merely "upright." God will give us the desires of our heart; whatever we ask, we shall receive.

According to **Proverbs 21:24 (NKJV)** *Proud and haughty man— "Scoffer" is his name; He acts with arrogant pride."* Lord your word says pride comes before a great fall. Lord my desire is to be more and more like you. Lord help me in the many areas of my life where I fall short and need more of you. Father in the name of Jesus, make me and mold me. Lord on my best days I still fall short, but Lord I am so thankful for your new mercies. Lord I am nothing without you, I need you more and more each day. **Proverbs 8:8-9** *⁸All the words of my mouth are with righteousness; nothing crooked or perverse is in them. ⁹They are all plain to him who understands, and right to those who find knowledge."*

❧ PRAYER ❧
✺✺✺✺✺

Lord, thank you for this new and exciting day. Thank you Lord for looking beyond my faults and seeing my needs. Lord, thank you for your love and daily protection. Lord, my desire is to live a life pleasing to you.

Father, you are mighty in all your ways. Lord I ask that you give me a discerning Spirit. Lord I ask that you continue to bless me with strength to do your will. Lord create in me a pure and clean heart and renew a right Spirit within me. Lord help me to love others the way that you love and care for me. Thank you oh Lord for seeing the best in me. Father mold me and shape me into the women you desire me to be. Lord in all that I do, I honor you. Thank you Lord for peace that only you can give. Thank, you, Lord, for friends and family. Lord, give us more insight into the things that concern you. Help us to be more, and more like you each day. Lord, bless and impart a spirit of discernment into the things that bring you honor. In Jesus' precious name, we pray. Amen

CAN THESE BONES LIVE?

***Ezekiel 37:1-3 (Holman Christian Bible)**, The hand of the LORD was on me, and he brought me out by the Spirit of the LORD and set me in the middle of the valley; it was full of bones. He led me all around them. There were a great many of them on the surface of the valley, and they were very dry. Then he said to me, "Son of man, can these bones live? I replied, "Lord God, only you know."*

If you were walking down the street and observed a minister of the gospel standing on the side of the road talking to a skeleton, what would you think? you would probably telephone the nearest mental hospital, wouldn't you? you would possibly assume this man was a menace to society.

Preaching to dry bones would seem like a waste of time and energy. But we sometimes forget the incredible power of God's Word. If God can speak matter into existence with just a word, make a man out of clay, or a woman out of a rib of a man, then it stands to reason that He can also cause the spiritually dead to hear. So don't lose hope, especially pastors and evangelists! We can preach to dry bones and witness results. God's Word is so potent and so powerful that it infuses new life into that which appears dead. When we are not serving God, we are like walking skeletons; however when God saves us we are new creatures in Him. We become alive.

Ezekiel 37:4-6 (Holman Christian Bible), *He said to me, Prophesy concerning these bones and say to them: Dry bones, hear the word of the Lord! This is what the Lord God says to these bones: I will cause breath to enter you, and you will live. I will put tendons on you, make flesh grow on you, and cover you with skin. I will put breath in you so you come to life. Then you will know I am Yahweh.* God continues to prove Himself to us over and over again.

Have you ever experienced being in a dry place? Of course! You know without a doubt you are saved and you know that God is with you and in you. BUT manifestation remains to be seen. Although you're in that place of dryness, do not stop praying. God will give strength. I believe the enemy attacks our mind. This is where the true battle begins. We cannot base kingdom principles on how we feel; our feelings come and go. When God's people preach the truth, it's going to cause a rattling. Things are going to happen. Sometimes it brings revival. At other times, it arouses opposition or persecution. Sometimes it does both! But I promise that when the truth is faithfully proclaimed, there's going to be a lot of shaking!

Peter tells us that growing in Christ is also a process with order. *2 Peter 1:5-8 (HCSB) ⁵For this very reason, make every effort to supplement your faith with goodness, goodness with knowledge, ⁶knowledge with self-control, self-control with endurance, endurance with godliness, ⁷godliness with brotherly affection, and brotherly affection with love. ⁸For if these qualities are yours and are increasing, they will keep you from being useless or unfruitful in the knowledge of our Lord Jesus Christ.*

In that dry place, know that our Father is still doing a work. And in that dry place, say what God says about you and your situations. *Ezekiel 37:10 (Holman Christian Bible), So I prophesied as He commanded me; the breath entered them, and they came to life and stood on their feet, a vast army.*

PRAYER
✸✸✸✸✸

Lord thank you for this Holy day. Thank you for life, health and strength. Oh most Holy and everlasting Father, thank you for last night's rest. Thank you for sending your angels to watch over me and my household as we slept during the night, then Oh Lord you touched us with your hand of love and woke us early this morning. Thank you Lord for your daily blessings and benefits. Father we love you and honor you. Lord, thank you for the gift of prayer. Sometimes, we all have experienced being in a dry place, but Lord we know that you are with us all the time. Lord, you spoke the earth into existence; how much more will you not do for your children? Lord, I know what it feels like to be in a dry season. Father, we know that no matter where we are on our journey with you, we are never alone. We have your promise, that you will never leave us nor will you forsake us. Lord, on this day, allow your children to feel the warmth and love of your embrace. These blessings we ask in Jesus' mighty name, Amen.

DON'T WORRY, BE HAPPY!

I've have heard others say, "I am not going to worry; I refuse to worry because worry does not change the situation". I too have said the same thing. From my experience, most people worry about their children, marriage, personal health, jobs and everything imaginable under the sun. I would like to expound on what worry is. "Worry" is excessive concern for something about which we can do absolutely nothing about. If we could do something about it, we would likely intervene and make the situation better. Although we can physically do nothing about the particular concern, we mull over it; ponder, and visualize the solution. The energy we expend in worrying is fruitless and accomplishes nothing because the word of God says cast our cares upon Him.

Luke 10:41- 42 (Holman Christian Bible) *The Lord answered her, "Martha, Martha, you are worried and upset about many things, but* *one thing is necessary. Mary has made the right choice, and it will not be taken away from her.* Jesus urges us not to worry about our basic needs of life, food and clothing, because life consists of more than these things. We are not given life because we deserve it, but because God is gracious enough to give it. God, being gracious enough to give us life, we can rest assure He will supply our every need.

The question is do we believe that God is who He says He is. If we do believe, then we must also believe that He will do what He says He will do. One tactic the enemy uses against us is worry. It begins in destroying our health. The thief uses a two-fold trap in destroying our minds through worry which does affect the body. Have you ever noticed that when worry is present, anxiousness takes up residence in your mind and it changes the way you feel? The enemy wants to keep us in a state of worry because there won't be freedom to pray the way we should. When I find myself in that negative state of mind, I immediately start humming a song and praying in my spirit. If I am at home, I put on songs of praise and immediately listen. Music and praise ushers us into the presence of our God. If you're going to worry, why pray? Ultimately worry will send us to early graves.

John 10:10 ((Holman Christian Bible), *A thief comes only to steal, and to kill, and to destroy. I have come that they may have life, and have it more abundantly.* So the cure for worry is humbling ourselves before God, casting our cares on Him, and trusting Him. Instead of making ourselves miserable trying to figure everything out on our own, God wants us to place our trust in Him and enter into His rest; totally abandoning ourselves to His care. **Psalm 85:8 (Holman Christian Bible),** *I will listen to what*

God will say; surely the Lord will declare peace to His people, and to His godly ones and not let them go back to foolish ways. God's example is our model for living; He has given us a map to follow in order to live a life of abundance. I believe we get into trouble when we deviate from His instructions and attempt to do contrary to His word.

Ecclesiastes 7:15-18 (Holman Christian Bible), *15In my futile life I have seen everything there is a righteous man who perishes in spite of his righteousness, and there is a wicked man who lives long in spite of his evil. 16Don't be excessively righteous, and don't be overly wise. Why should you destroy yourself? 17Don't be excessively wicked, and don't be foolish. Why should you die before your time? 18It is good that you grasp the one and do not let the other slip from your hand. For the one who fears God will end up with both of them.*

❧PRAYER❧
✽✽✽✽✽

Father thank you for this peaceful day. Thank you for your daily blessings, family and friends. Thank you Lord for the mind to serve you. Lord make me more like you. Create a pure heart in me and renew your Spirit in me. Father continue to show yourself mighty in my life. Lord help me to be a light in dark places. Lord I want to live a life that is pleasing and acceptable in your sight. Lord, thank you for peace that only you can give. Lord, thank you for your love and goodness to me. Lord there are days Father when I think of your love for us, I am always in awe. Lord, you look beyond our faults and see our needs. Lord, thank you for not giving us what we deserve. Thank you Father for being with us whether we are in the valley or on the mountain top. Lord, we know that worry does not come from you. Lord you said, if we keep our minds on you that you would keep us in perfect peace. Lord, we love you and honor your blessings. In your

Holy name, Amen.

IN OUR HEAVENLY FATHER, WE HAVE HOPE

I've desired and prayed for many things from the Lord. Some things I have prayed for have not materialize yet, but I have hope. Without hope, our heart will become sick. Without hope, we give in and give up. One of the things I hope and pray for is that God will save all of my family members. My eldest granddaughter who is 17 years old, shared with me last evening that she accepted the Lord in her heart this past Sunday. Hallelujah!! To God be the glory for all the good things He is doing and is going to do! God is allowing you and me to see the manifestation of prayers answered in this life. God has no respecter of person; we are all His creation. **Psalm 42:11 (Holman Christian Bible)** *Why am I so depressed? Why this turmoil within me? Put your hope in God, for I will still praise Him, my Savior and my God.* When our hope is completely in the Lord, we are not troubled when things go contrary to the way we plan. When we put our trust in God, we realize that He knows what is best for us. No matter what we must confront, God is our strength and shield.

John 15:16((Holman Christian Bible) *you did not choose me, but I have chosen you. I appointed you, that you should go out and produce fruit, and that your fruit should remain, so that whatsoever you ask the Father in My name, he will give you.* God loved us before we were ever conceived in our mother's womb.

Psalm 55:22(KJV) *Cast thy burden upon the LORD, and he shall sustain thee: he shall never suffer the righteous to be moved.* Without hope we give up and that is what the devil wants us to do. The Bible repeatedly tells us not to be discouraged or dismayed. God knows that we will not come through to victory if we get discouraged, so He always encourages us as we start out on a venture by saying to us, "I am with you." God wants us to be encouraged.

Matthew 7:7-8 (Holman Christian Bible) ⁷Keep asking, and it will be given to you. Keep searching, and you will find; Keep knocking, and the door will be opened unto you. ⁸For everyone who asks receives, and the one who searches finds; and to the one who knocks, the door will be opened. Sometimes the very things we are seeking and asking the Lord for are right at our finger tips, but we give up to easily. Some things we just have to wait on, because it is not God's time; or it could be as God is doing a work in us to prepare us for the things we are seeking Him for. I believe that some things come only by fasting and praying. ***Psalm 40:1 (KJV)*** *I waited patiently for the LORD; and he turned to me, and heard my cry for help.* The more we know God the more we will trust Him.

John 14:14 (Holman Christian Bible)*, If you ask Me anything in My name, I will do it.* When doubt tries to creep in our mind and attempt to overwhelm us, we have God's word. He will never leave us nor will He forsake us. Lord when times are hard and friends are few, I can rest in your faithfulness to me. Lord I know you want what's best for me and my family. Lord thank you for loving me, strengthening and thank you for all of your daily benefits. Lord I am so blessed to have you as my Father. Lord in all that I attempt to do, I will always honor you. Focus on God and His strength and not on the problem. Seek the Lord to aid you to increase the excellence and magnitude of your hope as you praise Him for His perfect powers. God is only a prayer away. He is waiting to help you.

PRAYER

Lord your awesome word is such consolation to us. Lord I have hidden your word in my heart. Thank you Heavenly Father for being an awesome father and friend to your children. Lord thank you for being our rock in a weary and dry place. Lord thank you for strength and power to do your will. Thank you dear father for the gift of hope. Thank you Lord for this wonderful day filled with expectation. Oh mighty God, thank you for giving your children hope. Lord, you are our hope. Lord, you are so good to us. Every day we need your grace and your mercy that is given to us freely. Lord, I could not imagine my life without you. Father your word is a lamp to my feet. Lord for the times I felt low and alone, your awesome Word reminded me that I am never alone and in you, I have hope for a brighter day. God, you are everything to me. Thank you Lord for loving me. God thank you for showing me so much compassion. Lord, look upon us this day. Continue your blessings to your children which is promised in your word. In Jesus mighty name we pray, Amen.

A SECRET STORM

Have you ever experienced being in a secret storm? A secret storm deals with struggles (current or past) that one has within oneself. Secret storms are embedded in the soul where no one knows perhaps except the Heavenly Father. Secret storms could be those mixed emotions and feelings of being less than another. It could be those private decisions we made without consulting Holy Spirit, or it could be past hurts we hold on to.

There are times when everything appears to be in the right place and things are moving at a regular pace, but then there are still those times when we are left on the outside; being too short to look in our own world of unstable grounds. We are so good at covering up and pretending that everything is okay. We are glamorously crafty at being what we think others want us to be. There is a deep hole within us that only God can fill, but we have to be honest about these flaws then submit.

Romans 7:15-25 (KJV) *For that which I do I allow not: for what I would, that do I not; but what I hate, that do I. If then I do that which I would not, I consent unto the law that it is good. Now then it is no more I that do it, but sin that dwelleth in me. For I know that in me (that is, in my flesh,) dwelleth no good thing: for to will is present with me; but how to perform that which is good I find not. For the good that I would I do not: but the evil which I would not, that I do. Now if I do that I would not, it is no more I that do it, but sin that dwelleth in me. I find then a law, that, when I would do good, evil is present with me. For I delight in the law of*

God after the inward man: But I see another law in my members, warring against the law of my mind, and bringing me into captivity to the law of sin which is in my members. O wretched man that I am! who shall deliver me from the body of this death? I thank God through Jesus Christ our Lord. So then with the mind I myself serve the law of God; but with the flesh the law of sin.

Pray without ceasing; God can do anything but fail. He knows our struggles. God is here, He is able to do what we cannot do for ourselves. Speak what God is saying about you and your situation. According to ***2 Corinthians 12: 9-10 (KJV)*** *⁹And he said unto me, My grace is sufficient for thee: for my strength is made perfect in weakness. Most gladly therefore will I rather glory in my infirmities, that the power of Christ may rest upon me. ¹⁰Therefore I take pleasure in infirmities, in reproaches, in necessities, in persecutions, in distresses for Christ's sake: for when I am weak, then am I strong.*

There is no failure in God; He is the beginning and He is the end, our God is light and in Him there is no darkness. Our God has all power in His hands, and He can do anything we desire Him to do in our lives. He is the perfect gentlemen; He will not invade our space. God is waiting to be invited into that place where it hurts the most. We must be willing to tell God all about our troubles, hurts, disappointments, and desires. He is willing to mend all the broken places in our lives if we will just let Him.

1 John:1-10 (KJV) *¹That which was from the beginning, which we have heard, which we have seen with our eyes, which we have looked upon, and our hands have handled, of the Word of life; ²For the life was manifested, and we have seen it, and bear witness, and shew unto you that eternal life, which was with the Father, and was manifested unto us; ³That which we have seen and heard declare we unto you, that ye also may have fellowship with us: and truly our fellowship is with the Father, and with his*

Son Jesus Christ. ⁴And these things write we unto you, that your joy may be full. ⁵This then is the message which we have heard of him, and declare unto you, that God is light, and in him is no darkness at all. ⁶If we say that we have fellowship with him, and walk in darkness, we lie, and do not the truth: ⁷But if we walk in the light, as he is in the light, we have fellowship one with another, and the blood of Jesus Christ his Son cleanseth us from all sin. ⁸If we say that we have no sin, we deceive ourselves, and the truth is not in us. ⁹If we confess our sins, he is faithful and just to forgive us our sins, and to cleanse us from all unrighteousness. ¹⁰If we say that we have not sinned, we make him a liar, and his word is not in us.

PRAYER

Father, in the name of Jesus, thank you for your continual love, goodness and mercy. Thank you for mending my brokenness. Father, thank you for being my rock and shelter in the time of my storms. Thank you Lord for looking beyond my faults and seeing my needs. Lord thank you for the ability to think with an open mind and heart. Lord thank you for strength to do your will. Thank you Heavenly Father for family and friends. Lord when I think of your goodness and your many, many blessings to me, my heart continues to thank you. Lord in our daily challenges and struggles help us to turn them all over to you. Lord mend all the broken hearts and make them new. Lord give us a smile where there is a frown, peace where there is confusion, and where there is pain, give us your divine comfort. Lord we all have secret storms we are faced with at one time or another. Lord continue to be a fence around us. Lord help us and guide your children in the right paths. Father, we need you every minute. These blessings we ask in your mighty name, Amen.

MISSION IMPOSSIBLE

We should celebrate God daily, but especially the week of His resurrection. He died and rose again with all POWER in His hands! We have that same power. Are you exercising His power in you? It is impossible to go wrong when we follow God's manual (The Bible). My sister said to me some time ago, "I know you are praying for me, because if you weren't, I believe my life would have ended a long time ago." I believe my sibling look to me as a mother figure, because our mother passed away when we were very young.

Philippians 2:13 *(KJV) For it is God which worketh in you both to will and to do of his good pleasure.* In some ways we are not skillful enough to persuade others of the power that lives on the inside of us, because we are not fully convinced of what God has already done in us. If we say we are filled with God's Holy Spirit and His power, then we need to walk boldly and confess it. I believe many times in our lives, we continue to petition God for the things He has already given us. We do not know who we are as children of the most High King.

1 Thessalonians 5: 16-18 *16Rejoice evermore. 17Pray without ceasing. 18In everything give thanks: for this is the will of God in Christ Jesus concerning you.* God's Word also tells us to pray for one another. We all stand in need of prayer. There is something about calling the name of Jesus that gives us hope, peace and reassurance. Jesus is the sweetest name I know, and I love calling on His name. Our identity in Christ is one of continual newness. We are new creations in Christ. Our lives should indicate that we are the same as Christ. The name "Christian" means literally "mimics of Christ." What an awesome privilege God has given to us. Do you really know who you are in Christ Jesus? Hallelujah, Hallelujah!

Our decision to obey God affects other people. When we disobey God that indeed affects other people. When we obey God, we are blessed as a result, and so is our loved ones. When we choose to disobey God, our loved ones suffer too. I believe that my life to a great extent remains because of the prayers of my grandparents and parents. We must pray continuously for ourselves, our children and family members. The enemy wants to sniff and devour us like wheat. ***Ephesians 6:18*** *(KJV) Praying always with all prayer and supplication in the Spirit, and watching thereunto with all perseverance and supplication for all saints;*

Ephesians 2:10 *(KJV) For we are his workmanship, created in Christ Jesus unto good works, which God hath before ordained that we should walk in them.* When God created us, He had a plan for our lives. That plan is to bring Him honor and glory. We are not our own but, were bought with a price and that was with His precious blood.

Matthew 10:16 *Look, I'm sending you out like sheep among wolves. Therefore be as shrewd as serpents and as harmless as doves.*

Acts 1:8 *But you will receive power when the Holy Spirit has come upon you, and you will be My witness in Jerusalem, in all Judea and Samaria, and to the ends of the earth.*

God has already equipped his children with everything we need to minister to others.

❍❰PRAYER❱❍
✻✻✻✻✻

Lord thank you for this special day. Thank you for another opportunity to lift your Holy and righteous name. Thank you for family and friends. Lord thank you for a mind to do your will. I love you Lord. Father my will is to please you, I honor you. Lord let my light shine so bright that others will see you in me. Lord help me to love like you love, and help others that are in need. My soul says thank you Jesus. Hallelujah, you are the most High King. Lord, when I think of you dying on the cross to save a sinner like me, I awe in your marvelous love. Lord, you made the conscience decision to lay down your life so that we could live. Lord, we could never re-pay what you have done and the love you have for your children. Lord, we want to live a life that brings you honor and glory. Lord, help us to remember the sacrifice you made on the cross for sinners like us. Lord, we are so grateful to you. We love you and praise you. In Jesus mighty name we pray, Amen.

ABOUT THE AUTHOR

Patricia S. Quillen – (1959) native of South Carolina is wife and mother of two and grandmother of seven. Patricia accepted the Lord Jesus Christ in her heart at an early age, under the leadership of the late Bishop JH Sherman. Patricia is a member of Abundant Life church, Dr. Carl Morris is her pastor. She is a member of family circles and serves on the praise team. Patricia is the founder of Caring Hearts of the Pee Dee. She accepted the call of God into ministry in August of 2010. Patricia has a heart for people especially hurting women and children.

Patricia received her undergraduate degree in Sociology from Francis Marion University, and a Master's degree in Mental Health Counseling from Webster University in Myrtle Beach, SC. She received certification in Christian Counseling from Chapman University, School of theology, under the leadership of Pastor/Apostle Lavern Chapman. Patricia is a notary republic of South Carolina. "Patricia's favorite bible verse is Philippians 4:13 I can do all things thru Christ which strengthens me" Her motto is If she can help somebody as I travel thru this life then, her living will not be in vain; let go and let God.

www.ingramcontent.com/pod-product-compliance
Lightning Source LLC
Chambersburg PA
CBHW020935090426
42736CB00010B/1148